This is more than a book—this is a journey! It is a journey into the heart of God, communicated in a simple, yet profound, way. Evelyn Lang has penned her heart and will clearly connect with those who hunger for a deeper, more spiritually substantive relationship with the Father. I commend this journey to you and suggest a complete saturation in the truths found along the way.

—RANDALL E. HOWARD
FOUNDER AND PRESIDENT, GREATER HOPE INTERNATIONAL
SENIOR PASTOR, FAITH COMMUNITY CHURCH
VICTORVILLE, CALIFORNIA

With a fresh, uncomplicated, yet compassionate way of communicating road stops along man's spiritual journey, Evelyn Lang has encouraged the reader to look at the everyday and listen to what God may be saying through it. A relaxed, yet enduring, read, these lessons will stay with you.

—STEVE AND CHRIS KINON
COFOUNDERS, DREAM WEAVERS INTERNATIONAL

I have the great privilege to recommend to you Evelyn Lang's *Lessons I Learned From the Lord.* If you have ever wondered about God's timing in your life, this book is for you. If you have been tried and tested, and thought that God had forgotten about you, then this book is for you. You will find encouragement, challenge, inspiration, and most of all a sense that God has a wonderful plan and purpose for your life. Evelyn speaks from personal experience and a close walk with God. The lessons she shares are time tested and proven. This a must-read for all believers!

—DR. J. TOD ZEIGER
EMBASSY INTERNATIONAL
MARYVILLE, TENNESSEE

"From this lesson we are warned...." (1 Cor. 10:6). Paul goes to great length to not only draw lessons from the Old Testament saints, but to also share in graphic detail his own experiences and the lessons learned. Evelyn Lang has rendered an invaluable service to the body of Christ in *Lessons I Learned From the Lord*. Her transparency in sharing and the life applications drawn will provide inspiration and guidance for the reader whether a new Christian or a mature saint. We commend these lessons to every reader and join her in prayer for the widest circulation possible.

—CRAWFORD AND DORATHY RAILEY
ATLANTA HEALING HOUSE

Lessons I Learned From the Lord is one book I would recommend if you are wanting to take steps toward learning how the supernatural nature of God interacts and speaks through multifaceted means in our lives and how these events mature us so we can aid others. Evelyn Lang has clearly and simply addressed what many Christians make unnecessarily difficult. I believe that God wants us to know His ways. This books aids us in growing in that knowledge.

—JOHN PAUL JACKSON
STREAMS MINISTRIES INTERNATIONAL
NORTH SUTTON, NEW HAMPSHIRE

Evelyn has had exciting personal revelation in life's journey with the Lord Jesus Christ. In her book she is transparent, simply speaking from her heart. This book will challenge you to develop a deeper relationship with the Lord.

—GARY PANEPINTO
FOUNDER, UPWARD CALL MINISTRY
EXECUTIVE PASTOR, THE CHURCH OF GRACE AND PEACE
TOMS RIVER, NEW JERSEY

Lessons
I learned
from
the Lord

Evelyn Lang

CREATION
HOUSE
A STRANG COMPANY

LESSONS I LEARNED FROM THE LORD by Evelyn Lang
Published by Creation House
A Strang Company
600 Rinehart Road
Lake Mary, Florida 32746
www.creationhouse.com

Scripture quotations are from the King James Version of the Bible.

Cover design by Terry Clifton

Library of Congress Control Number: 2005936911
International Standard Book Number: 1-59185-985-9

First Edition

06 07 08 09 — 987654321
Printed in the United States of America

Dedication

This book is dedicated to:

- God, for giving me the privilege of writing this book for Him. To God be the glory.

- My husband, Bill, whose loving support, encouragement, and help I could always depend on. Thank you—I love you.

- Rose, who listened to God and spoke His Word to tell me I would be writing a book. God bless you.

- Carol, a mighty vessel of God whose word brought the life-changing revelation to me that God heard my prayers. May God bless you and continue to give you much "fruit."

Acknowledgments

 would like to thank all the editors at Strang Communications for having faith in an "unknown author" and taking a chance on this book. I would especially like to thank Allen Quain for his encouraging words and support in making this book possible. I could not put a value on his knowledge and experience in helping me. Many thanks to all the staff at Strang, Creation House, the copy editors, cover designers, and those in marketing, who have worked so hard on bringing it to completion. I want to give special thanks to Ginny Maxwell, who answered dozens of questions with patience and understanding.

Thanks and love to my husband, Bill, who had the "patience of a saint" and was always there to help me in any way I needed. Regardless of how busy you were, you always made the time to help me. My love and gratitude to you could never be expressed in words.

I would also like to thank my pastors, Dr. J. Patrick Fiore and his lovely wife, Rev. Susan Fiore, for believing in me and giving me the courage to submit this book for publication. You will never know how much your support meant to me. Your friendship is a treasured blessing, and it is a privilege to be in your "flock."

Foreword

*T*o know Evelyn Lang is to love Evelyn Lang. From the first time I was introduced to "Ev" (as she is affectionately known), I fell in love with her kindness, gentleness, and humility. In fact, I asked myself if someone as Christlike as Ev could really be the genuine thing. Guess what? I found out over the last couple of years that she is the real deal!

From the moment we met, I could tell she was a woman filled with the compassion of God for other people. She is a real "mom," not only in the natural, but also in the spiritual sense of being a "mother in Israel."

She is a woman who regularly communes with God and is one of the most "prophetic" people I have ever known. I have the privilege of serving as her pastor, and sometimes I have to help her to see that although God is the One who gives all gifts, He also needs to have available people to flow through. Sometimes Ev is so deflective in being careful to give all of the honor and glory to God that I have to remind her that God can only accomplish what He does because she continually says "yes" to Him!

When Ev approached me to write the Foreword for this book, the first thing that she did was to apologize for the fact that she really was not a writer and moreover disliked and avoided writing from the time she was a child. I was then unsure of what I was going to read and how I was going to respond to her, especially if the book wasn't very good. (Being a pastor, you always need to find the silver lining in any situation to be an encouragement to people.)

I must admit that once I opened up the manuscript and began reading the table of contents I was absolutely amazed at what I was seeing. Beginning with the chapter titles, and concluding with the gentle invitation to follow Christ, I was amazed at the ability Ev had to communicate in the most simple, yet profound way, the mysteries of God.

You will laugh and cry as you read the stories, illustrations, and object lessons that are so clearly insights and wisdom only God could give someone listening to what He was saying. You will have a challenging decision as to whether you want to read the entire book in one sitting or whether you want to read a chapter a day so that you can absorb some of the life-changing principles found in this book. It will challenge you in ways you have never been challenged before. *Lessons I Learned From the Lord* will create a hunger and an intimacy that you never dreamed could happen to you. Fasten your spiritual seatbelt, and get ready for a ride that you will never forget. And not only won't it hurt, but it also will give you feelings of warmth and intimacy with God that will carry you to the next level in your spiritual journey.

—J. PATRICK FIORE, PHD
CEO AND FOUNDER OF
APRECIS GROUP LEADERSHIP SERVICES
SENIOR PASTOR, CHRISTIAN LIFE CENTER
WEST MILFORD, NEW JERSEY

Contents

Introduction

As a child I was brought up in a small church, and I loved the Lord. However, it was never taught nor was there any evidence that God still did miracles. It was never taught that Satan still attacks Christians. It was like we were getting a history lesson. I prayed to God, but never really expected to hear Him. I knew He could answer our prayers, but I just thought that the answer would come with circumstances—I did not think I could hear His answer in prayer. I certainly didn't expect to hear His voice. When my husband and I got married, we raised our children in the same denomination. Then one day I turned on the television and saw a Christian program. I was hearing about God healing and doing miracles today! I wanted to know more, and a hunger developed. I wasn't satisfied with religion or Sunday Christianity. I realized

I could have a personal relationship with God—but how was I to get it? I had been a Christian all my life, yet I realized there were so many things I didn't know. I couldn't wait for that TV program to come on every day.

Then a neighbor asked me to go to a Woman's Aglow meeting. The speaker was a pastor from a Pentecostal, Holy Spirit-filled church in our area. I knew that was where we had to go. There, I heard words of knowledge and prophecy. It was the start of my journey. Then at another Aglow meeting, someone prayed over me and told me that I had the gift of the word of knowledge. I had desired it, but was blocking it out of fear. I still did not understand, even though God had been giving me revelation and wisdom. So I started to read books and listen to tapes to help me understand and learn. Then one thing happened that was life changing. During worship in church one Sunday, I kept asking God, "Where is my light?"

During our greeting time, I went to say hello to a friend who was strong in the Lord and was used mightily in the gifts of the Holy Spirit. The anointing of God was still upon her when she said, "Your sweetness is your light!" I had not told her what I was praying, and for the first time I knew that God heard *me*—that He loved me enough to answer! From that time on, my prayer life changed. I prayed, but I also listened for the answer. I started to communicate with God. I was getting that personal relationship with God and from that came the gifts of the Holy Spirit. That was many years ago, and it has been an incredible journey. I have learned many lessons along the way. A few years ago someone else prophesied over me that I was going to write a book. This was especially amazing to me because even as a child I would agonize over having to write essays in school. I didn't even like writing letters because I never knew what to say. I'm still like that. Yet somewhere deep inside, I had always thought it would be wonderful to write a book. After that prophecy, I went home and prayed and asked God about it. I asked Him, if He wanted me to write a book, what would the name be? I had no idea of what kind of book it would be. I immediately got the name *Lessons I Learned From the Lord.* I told God that I wasn't a writer. (Of course He already knew.) He told me that that was why I was to be the one to write it—I would know that it wasn't me simply for that reason. I told Him that this would have to be His book and that He would have to give me the words to write. I know that I'm nothing special—just a little ol' me that God has used as His vessel. And God can use you, too. So here it is: *Lessons I Learned From the Lord.*

Chapter 1

"Hello, this is the Lord. Is anyone listening?"

everal years ago I wondered why, as a Christian, I wasn't hearing God's voice. After all, I was praying, but it was a one-way prayer. I would wonder what Jeremiah 33:3 meant when it said, "Call unto me, and I will answer thee, and show thee great and mighty things, which thou knowest not." I never knew what God had planned for me. I wanted to know God's will in and for my life. I wondered especially because God says in His Word, "My sheep know My voice." I would ask God, "I'm your sheep—why don't I hear your voice?" Well, it wasn't because He wasn't talking. I just wasn't listening. It wasn't until I spent time in prayer *communicating* with God that I starting hearing. It took time learning that just as I speak to a friend, that's how I should to talk to God. We can ask Him questions about what we should do in a situation, or how He feels, and He will answer. You see, many times we're "fast-food" Christians, and we pray by listing our needs like we're ordering food at a fast-food restaurant. When we're done "ordering," we wait in silence to hear something profound when we haven't even asked God a question for Him to respond to. At times we don't even wait for an answer! Many times we have so much clutter in our minds that we don't have room for anything else. We sometimes just need to take out the clutter and focus on the Lord.

God created Adam and Eve so that He could have man to commune with. He would walk and talk with them in the garden. They lost that fellowship by sin. Sometimes it's sin that actually causes us to shut God out because we really don't *want* to hear from Him. Adam and Eve did the same thing when they hid from God after eating the forbidden fruit. We're afraid He will convict us of our sin. But even those Christians walking in obedience sometimes are not hearing due to lack of knowledge, just being busy, rattling off prayers quickly, or not spending the time to get to *know* Him. Some don't even realize or expect that He will talk to us. God wants us to *ask* Him things. Yes we can come before Him and ask *for* things, but He also wants us to ask Him *about* things. Once you start doing this, He starts revealing Himself to you and you start learning about Him, His ways, His heart, and His goodness. God created man to be able to talk to Him, but the majority of people don't think this is possible or even normal to be able to have conversations with God. We are happy when we have a friend to talk to. God is happy to have friends to talk to also. People need communication. That's why solitary confinement in prison is punishment. God needs communication with His people, too. But many have put Him in solitary confinement simply because they think that God does not or will not speak to them. Some were never told that He does. They think that hearing from God is a great mystery. This is wrong thinking that is passed down from generation to generation. It starts with one person's wrong thinking and is passed on to others until the misconception becomes more popular and is accepted as truth. It continues to spread and becomes bigger and more accepted as more and more people believe it. It's like a snowball going downhill, picking up more snow as it travels. Belief systems get started that way. Once established, traditions are hard to break. If people don't know that they can have conversations with God it won't even enter their minds to try to speak to Him expecting to hear Him answer. God longs to speak to His children, but many don't know that they can communicate with Him. He wants His children to know Him in a personal way. Prayer is not one-sided. Prayer is often thought of as lifting up our needs and then that's that. People will talk to God, but don't wait for Him to respond and talk to them. They don't even give God a chance to speak. It's as though they were talking to a wall, and because they don't wait to hear from God, they think that's the way it is. How would we feel if we were with a friend who talked continually and we didn't get a chance to say a word? How would we feel if this happened all the time when we were with this person? How would we feel if we were not even expected to respond? It would not be a fulfilling relationship. There would be no "give and take" of conversation. It would only be a speech. God listens to speeches, but He wants more. He wants relationship. He wants fellowship. He wants people to know how He feels and what He thinks. He wants them to *know* Him.

Sometimes God gives me an analogy to help me to understand what He's telling me. He showed me telegraph wires and explained that telegraph wires carry words and messages to people. He said that He has an open telegraph wire—an open line to His people. They can talk to Him at all times. All they have to do is call upon Him, and He will answer. (See Jeremiah 33:3.) This is because of relationship. When we have a close relationship with someone, we can call them anytime—day or night—and they will answer. We cannot do this with an acquaintance, but we can with a close friend. Jesus wants that close friendship with everyone, but so many only talk to Him on Sunday. How can they know Him by spending only an hour a week with Him? And even then, their minds are on other things. But God's telegraph lines are always open—it's their receivers that are dead. They have turned them off. They don't believe God will converse with them. But God wants us to turn our receivers on, start talking to Him and see if He won't answer! He will talk to us—it's not unusual. To think otherwise is to believe a lie.

God has many children, but not all know Him. Many say they are Christians, but they don't spend time with Him, or talk to Him except in times of need or if they want something. We can believe someone exists, but that doesn't mean we know him. For example, we can believe that Queen Elizabeth is real and that she exists, but just believing that fact doesn't mean that we know her personally or that she knows us. We only know *of* her. Many people who say they are Christians know of God, but they don't really know Him. They don't have a personal relationship with Him. It must make God feel cut off from them. They may go to church on Sunday and worship Him and even want to be in His presence, but then Monday it's back to work as usual, and God is put aside. People think that the only thing that cuts them off from God is unconfessed sin. It is true that sin separates, but it is busyness that prevents a close relationship with God. It's when people don't talk to God that makes Him feel cut off from them. It's when they go about their lives during the week with business as usual, not thinking of Him unless they have a need. People don't always have to be in a prayer closet or church to connect with Him. All they have to do is talk to Him. They can do this at all times, wherever they are or whatever they are doing. You see, the Sabbath is more for us than for God. It is the day of rest and refreshing. But for God, if we only take the time to be with Him on Sunday and forget about Him the rest of the week, it must feel like when an elderly person has many visitors on Sunday but is alone the rest of the week. If people would just speak to God at all times, whatever they are doing, their lives would be so much better. God wants us to desire Him and crave being with Him. He wants us to need Him, but He wants to be desired even when there is no need.

One day as I was praying, I believe God showed me His heart for His people, and how He desires for them to come to Him and to get to know Him. He showed me that He loves His people—yet He mourns for them, for they do not know Him. His heart aches because he wants to reveal Himself to them. He wants them to draw near to Him. He wants to care for them and protect them and bless them—yet they do not know this. If only they would come to Him—He is real. If only they would know that He is more real than what their senses can touch, or see, or smell, or taste. Why do they go about their business without even a thought of Him? Don't they know His desires for them? He is the answer, yet they do not seek Him. His heart aches for them. He loves them, yet they do not know. Some do not even know to come and ask His help. He wants so much for His children, yet they do not look to Him. God's desire is for us to seek Him out, to communicate with Him, to hear His voice, to know His heart.

God speaks to us in many ways. I used to think that I actually needed to hear a thunder-like voice and if I didn't, it couldn't be God. Only when I became "tuned in" did I realize the many ways in which God speaks to us. Many times during prayer I'll get a revelation, or an understanding of something that I never thought of before. Sometimes I'll read a verse of Scripture, and although I've read it many times before, I will "see" something in it that will answer something I've been praying about and reveal to me what I couldn't see before. Sometimes it's a knowing in your spirit, and sometimes God lets you "feel" His heart, His love, or His sorrow. Sometimes I'll be awakened at night with words coming into my mind before I'm fully awake, or sometimes it's a dream. Sometimes He'll speak a word through someone else, or through a circumstance. God speaks to us in many ways, if we're attuned to His Spirit. One day in the very beginning when I was just discovering all the different ways God speaks to us, I was doing the dishes when I got a "sense" that I should turn on the television to TBN. I didn't respond to this sense right away, however. In fact, I told myself that I would turn it on as soon as I finished the dishes. The urgency got stronger. So I thought, *Well, I'll just finish this ladle.* (I was arguing with myself, I thought, as to why I couldn't do it!) But by then, the feeling became so strong that I gave in to it and turned on TBN. I turned it on just in time to hear a word that I knew was for me! One minute later and it would have been too late—I would have missed it. How many times do we miss out on what God has for us by ignoring the Holy Spirit's prompting? The more we listen, the more we recognize His voice. The more we get tuned in, the more He reveals Himself to us. God's Word says that to him who has, more will be given. (See Matthew 25:29.) We need to ask God to reveal

Himself to us, and ask Him what He would like to tell or teach us today. I have also found that God will usually confirm what He tells us. This could be a confirmation through Scripture, a word from another, a dream, maybe even a circumstance.

God has also shown me that during prayer, we sometimes need to be silent and just be in His presence and "connect" with Him. It's when we are in a state of such worship that we don't always need or want to talk in His presence. Just as a husband and wife have times when they can be together and don't need to say a word, but can look into each others eyes and feel such love, such a spiritual connection as one—that God also wants us to feel so connected to Him that we can bask in His presence and feel His love without having said a word.

There are times when we hear a lot, and then we may go though times when we don't hear as much. We should not be discouraged or think that God has pulled away or that maybe we have "lost" the ability to hear from Him. God's love for us is constant. It doesn't ebb and flow like the tide does; it doesn't blow this way and that way like the wind does; it doesn't depend on how we feel. We should not let our feelings control our faith. He is always with us. I believe we have growth spurts and resting times. Just as a child's growth can be in spurts, so it is with us as we grow in our Christian walk. Resting times, I believe, are when we absorb what we've learned and are being purified so that we can go to a higher level. You never lose what you had when you go through these resting times—in fact, these times may be when God is doing His greatest work in you so that you can grow some more. I see it as a stepladder, always climbing up in the process of being perfected in Him. Sometimes I think that God hides from us so that we will seek Him more.

Most of us hear the Holy Spirit's still, small voice, but don't realize it is He. We wonder if it isn't our own thoughts, especially when God speaks to us in our minds. It seems to sound like us. But recognizing God's voice isn't like recognizing voices in the natural. There is no sound. I think that's where many people get confused. Realizing that it is God's thought instead of your own takes practice. It's during those times when you get a revelation, and you wonder how you could have possibly thought of it. It's a sense, or a fleeting thought, or a knowing, or a surprise thought, or all of them. God will give us instructions and answers not thought of or known to us. It very often does not sound any different than we sound, yet we would not or could not have thought of it on our own.

When God speaks audibly, there is no question it is God, but that isn't as common. Most of the time I believe God speaks to us inwardly, and, because we are in Him and He in us, it comes into our minds. People sometimes have trouble realizing that everything that comes into their minds is not their thought. Once they realize this, they get "fine-tuned" as to what's coming from God and what's coming from them. That's what meant by recognizing His voice. They will know that it wasn't their thought.

The enemy can put thoughts in our minds. We need to know this and also recognize when it is the enemy. If we don't, we can be put under guilt and condemnation and chastise ourselves for having such awful thoughts. We will tend to blame ourselves instead of the enemy. Then we sometimes will block out all thoughts, even God's, for fear of the bad thoughts coming back in. That's exactly what the enemy wants, for then he can shut down your mind from hearing God. Baby Christians who don't know the enemy's tactics have a hard time with this. This is especially true for those who God wants to use prophetically. Satan will do anything to stop the prophetic. And his tactic is to attack their minds. Unfortunately he's very often successful because people have a hard time understanding where these thoughts are coming from. One way we can know if it is the enemy's thought is if the thoughts are thoughts that you don't want, or your fears. Because they are thoughts that we don't want, we should realize that they are not our thoughts. We must not feel guilty as if they were. It's just that simple. Another way to discern where a thought is coming from is the fruit of the thought. It doesn't matter if the words themselves seem all right. If they give peace, it is God. If they bring fear or guilt and condemnation, it is the enemy. Even when God corrects, it is not condemning—it does not produce fear. That is the test of everything—the fruit it produces. What kind of fruit does the person's life produce, a thought produce or a prophecy produce? There is a saying that the proof is in the pudding— actually, it's really in the fruit! When words are not of God, they are inedible. They will not digest easily. We will have an uncomfortable feeling in our stomach. God's words are like honey. Even words that convict us will be coated with honey (love) so that we can swallow them easier. It is never a bitter pill. God's Word says, "My people are destroyed for lack of knowledge" (Hosea 4:6). We also must not worry that God will think that those thoughts are ours, for in Psalm 139:2, it says, "Thou knowest my downsitting and mine uprising, thou understandest my thought afar off."

The battle is in the mind. Yet most people will just give up—it's too hard to fight, and there are those who don't even realize there's a battle going on. It's so important for God's people not to give up when the attacks come. The more the attacks come, the more God wants to speak to them and use them; otherwise, why would Satan bother? These mind battles are not unusual or uncommon. People are just afraid to talk about them, and this unknowingly perpetuates the lies of the enemy. The only way to defeat these lies is to expose them. Tell the enemy you know that it is he that is doing it when these unwanted thoughts come in and rebuke them! As he is exposed, he'll eventually give up, unless you give up first. He wants to wear you out. The key is to just keep rebuking him and declaring God's Word. In Philippians 4:8, it says, "Finally brethren, whatsoever things are true, whatsoever things are honest, whatsoever things are just, whatsoever things are pure, whatsoever things are lovely, whatsoever things are of good report; if there be any virtue, and if there be any praise, think on these things." Many Christians are agonizing over the enemy's thoughts, thinking they are their own, therefore claiming them, and being afraid to talk about it for fear of what people will think of them. Satan has them in a net. Break through, rebuke the thought, and move on! Then your mind will be open to hear God's thoughts—His voice. And you will learn to recognize His thoughts, His voice, from your own and from the enemy's.

In the Bible, God tells us to look for His coming. It's the same with His words. He is always instructing and speaking to His people, but if they are not looking for His voice, it goes right by them without them realizing it. Their answer was there all the while. If you're not "tuned in" to God's voice, you won't hear. There are many radio stations, but you have to be "tuned in" to one to hear it. If you are walking in God's Spirit, then you are thinking about Him and then you won't miss His coming. For your heart is with Him. If you are walking in His Spirit, then you will also look for His instructions and won't miss His voice. How many times can we look back and say, "Something told me not to do this, but I ignored it, did it, and got hurt in some way"? As an example, suppose that you get a strong impression that if you climb up that stepladder with those floppy slippers, you're going to fall. But you ignore that small, still voice and reason in your mind that you'll be careful, and then up you go, only to trip and fall. And all the while the Holy Spirit is saying, "Don't do that! Danger! Stop!" On the other hand if we heed that voice, and change into our shoes, all is well. One day I was driving down a road by my house that I travel on most days. It has a blind curve that has a street coming out right after the curve. Most days I go around the curve carefully, but this particular day, as I started to enter the curve, I got the impression that I needed to be more careful than usual and slow down, because a car was going to come flying out of that street. I did obey that warning and sure enough, as I got to the street, a car did come flying out. If I had not slowed down more than usual, I would have been hit. Most people don't realize that they're hearing from the Holy Spirit when these impressions come.

Sometimes the Holy Spirit will warn us and tell us not to do something, and we don't know why. We need to obey and not question. He will tell us what we need to know for the moment and may reveal the rest to us at a later time. Don't think that because you haven't gotten the reason why you should not do it, that it can't be from God. You don't have to know everything for it to be God. He very often reveals things to us in part. He may not want us to know the reason why right away, or it may be that He just wants to tell us what we need to know for that moment. Sometimes we can't handle knowing everything at once—we should just obey. Imagine how the Holy Spirit must feel when He's warning us, and because of our limited reasoning, or because we don't know why and can't validate the reason we shouldn't do it through our human thinking, do it anyway. God helped me understand this by giving me the example of a parent watching as their small child starts to put his hand on the hot stove burner. They shout to the child, "NO, don't touch that," but are not able to stop the child in time. The horrors of watching their child get burned! How we must, in trusting our own intellect, do the same to the Holy Spirit. I'm sure He watches in horror as we ignore His warnings and eventually get hurt. If we would just listen to His small, still voice, and not block it out because we don't know the why's, we would save ourselves a lot of trouble and pain. What stubborn children we can be! The enemy will try to tell you that because you don't know why, your "feeling" isn't valid. He'll say to us, "Oh go ahead, there is no reason not to do it; it won't hurt you"—just like he did to Eve in the garden. Don't believe it! Why do we tend to believe our own logic or the enemy's lies and not the Holy Spirit, even when He's shouting danger to us? We need to train ourselves to listen and hear what He's telling us and then obey.

To summarize, God is speaking to His people all the time; however, we're not always listening for His voice. Unless we are listening, His Word will go by unnoticed. Many times, people just don't expect to be able to have conversations with God. Sometimes these people may hear during times of crisis because at those times they expect to hear from Him. But for most other times, they may feel they are insignificant or their problems too small to "bother" God. They don't realize He is accessible to us at all times. They think He doesn't want to come and just talk to them. How can we His people get to know Him if we put Him at a distance? We over-reverence

Him to the point of where we don't think we can talk to Him, except in times of great need. But even though He is God Almighty, He does not consider himself too great to be near His people. He desires to be right with His people—to fellowship and to communicate with us just like He did with Adam. However we sometimes tend to think of Him as a King that isolates Himself from His people, except in times of emergency. When will we receive Him as our friend? When will we allow Him in our circle of friends? He wants to be walking and talking with His people. Yes, He is our Savior and King, but He also wants to be our friend. (See John 15:15.) He wants an intimate friendship with each one of His people. He wants us to tell Him our cares for today, our hopes for tomorrow. He wants to rejoice with us in our victories and be there for us in times of sorrow. When we realize this, and let Him in, we will never be alone.

Breakfast of God's Champions

Just as our bodies need food to sustain us, so does our spirit. For we are spirit—we just happen to live in an earthly body of flesh. Our flesh needs natural foods to function properly and give us energy. Our spirit needs spiritual food, bread from heaven, which is the Word of God. Most of us have "starving spirits" which is why we feel "empty" and unfulfilled. We feel like something is missing in our lives. We overfeed our bodies and make them fat while our spirits shrink from malnourishment. We spend fortunes on supplements and health clubs to take care of our bodies—and we should take care of them. God wants us to, for our bodies are our earthly houses and the temple of the Holy Spirit. However, we need balance. Our spiritual body needs to be taken care of as well. Where do our spiritual "supplements" and exercise come from? They come from spending time in prayer and reading God's Word, which is the bread of life. It is bread for the soul.

One day while I was in prayer, God was showing me a rose. It was soft, delicate, and beautiful. He showed me what happens when it becomes dried out. It becomes hard and brittle. He told me that it gets dried out when its nourishment is cut off. He then gave me a comparison that we are like that rose. We need to get our nourishment, which is fellowship and communion with Him, to remain soft, delicate, and beautiful. He showed me that when there is no fellowship with Him, our spiritual nourishment is cut off, and we become hardened. We become hard-hearted. Just as the rose needs water, we need His living water.

Isaiah 55:1–2 states, "Ho, every one that thirsteth, come ye to the waters, and he that hath no money; come ye, buy, and eat; yea, come, buy wine and milk without money and without price. Wherefore do ye spend money for that which is not bread? And your labour for that which satisfieth not? Hearken diligently unto me, and eat ye that which is good, and let your soul delight itself in fatness"

In John 4, Jesus is talking to a Samaritan woman at Jacob's well. He tells her that people soon become thirsty after drinking this water. But the water He gives is living water. Whoever drinks this water will never thirst again.

I have found that whenever I get too busy to take that time in the morning to be in God's presence, the day just doesn't go as well. And if it becomes several days, my spirit gets weak, and the enemy can attack more easily. By spending time with God and reading His Word in the morning before your day begins, you are feeding your spirit the Breakfast of God's Champions.

Chapter 2

Burn the Vegetable Soup
and Clean the Pot

*W*hen God spoke "vegetable soup" to me, I knew He was going to teach me something by example. A wonderful writing, *Chicken Soup for the Soul* feeds your soul with warm and fuzzy thoughts, which we all need. Vegetable soup, however, is much different. When my grandmother had only a few potatoes, maybe some leftover carrots and peas and some other vegetables, not enough left over for a meal, she would make soup. God showed me that when we are "new creations" in Christ, He "cleans" us up. Sometimes though, we have "leftovers" buried so deep in our hearts that we either don't realize that they are there, or we don't want to admit or deal with them. There may be a little leftover piece of pride, or jealousy, maybe a little piece of bitterness or unforgiveness hidden inside.

As new baby Christians, we get along with leaving them buried, but as we mature and as God wants to use us as His vessels, we need to let God's fire "burn" these leftovers in our soup and clean the pot, which is our heart. How do we know these leftovers are hidden away? After years, they may rear their ugly heads—and we're surprised because in our pride we thought we couldn't have these feelings. God will bring them to the surface so that we can deal with them and get rid of them. God will put us through the fire to burn these impurities so we can have a pure heart, He can bring us closer to Him, and He can use us. It reminds me of the song "Refiner's Fire," which tells about needing to go through the fire in order to be holy, set apart unto God. Going through fire is not easy—in fact, it's uncomfortable to deal with these issues and sometimes down right painful. Occasionally, as God exposes these "leftovers" to us, we want to run from Him and bury them back again, only to deal with them at another time. We chastise ourselves and feel like failures and wonder how God could love us when we still have these things inside. We tend to want to run from God because our sin makes us ashamed to be in His presence. This is exactly what the enemy wants and he will put us under even more guilt and condemnation if we let him. However, the very reason why God exposes these things to us is because He wants us to run *to* Him with it, confess it, repent, and move on. It's exactly the opposite of what we think. It's because of God's love for us that He exposes it. He wants to draw us close to Him, and therefore we must be holy, because He is holy. His desire is that we become closer to Him, and so He purges us. This is so that we can bear more fruit. (See John 15:1–6.)

God had given me a comparison of this process. It's just like when we get a splinter. It's uncomfortable while it's there, painful to remove, but it feels so much better when it's gone. We need to die to these things of the flesh in order to become more like Jesus. It's a continual process of dying, learning and growing. Paul spoke of himself dealing with this is Romans 7:15.

We sometimes fear God's anger when it's because of His love for us that He refines us. This fear may be because of our upbringing. We may have had parents and people in authority punishing us severely, not forgiving us right away, speaking harsh words over us, holding grudges, or people that keep reminding us of our past failures. It's hard for us to accept and realize that our Heavenly Father is not like that. God is not mad at us. As I was contemplating this, I felt God's sadness and heart for His People. I believe He was showing me that He does not want His people to fear Him—reverence yes, but not fear in the way people understand the word. He wants His people to know that He is God Almighty, and He wants them to know His great love, His tenderness, His care of and for them   if they will allow it. He wants them to come to Him for help and *expect* Him to be loving and kind. He has so much love for His people, yet many don't know it. Their hearts may have been hardened to Him because of fear, because they think He is harsh and full of punishment, when instead His mercy is always there! His heart breaks because He wants them to know His love.

The enemy would put in fear, to accuse and destroy—don't listen! Jesus did not come to condemn, but to save. Run to Him—He can help! Just ask Him and see what He won't do for you! But who will tell people? Who will listen? He weeps, weeps, for His people that have hardened their hearts against Him. They believe the lies of the enemy. Close you ears to the enemy—don't listen, don't listen to him. But open your hearts to God. Receive His love. Be delivered, be healed—He is the Source. Walk in the freedom that His love brings. He is Love.

We also sometimes want to hold onto these "leftovers." After all, we think, *I have a right to be angry or bitter. Look what they did to me.* These feelings may be buried or not. However, God doesn't care about the reason—He cares about the result. Unforgiveness, anger, or any other leftover, no matter how "justified," will prevent you from walking in God's fullness, freedom, and all that He has for you! We tend to want to embrace our leftover and hold onto it. We need to bring it to the cross, plead the blood of Jesus and leave it there. As was stated before, it is a trick of Satan to keep reminding us of our failures and to put us under guilt and condemnation. He comes to steal , kill and destroy. (See John 10:10.) So often we believe the enemy's lies and think that God will be mad at us. It's human nature to always believe the worst. But in the Spirit, it is so different—just the opposite. So we battle it out and feel the struggle. At these times we need to realize what Jesus did for us on the cross, and declare His Word and promises. There is now no condemnation for those in Christ Jesus. (See Romans 8:1.) If we were perfect, He would not have had to die for us. God looks at us through the blood of Jesus. And He looks at our hearts. A broken heart, a repentant heart melts the heart of God—an arrogant, prideful heart does not.

The heart (spirit) is command central in us. It motivates everything we do. The natural heart pumps blood (life) throughout the body. If there are harmful bacteria in the blood, it poisons (affects) every part of the body. The spiritual heart pumps life throughout the spiritual body. If it has been poisoned by bitterness, resentment, etc., there will be spiritual sickness. The result will be that these people will be weak and will not be effective for God's kingdom. It affects their whole lives negatively. But when people have the fruit of God's Spirit within them, they are spiritually strong. They are healthy and can be used for God's kingdom purposes.

The way to get rid of these spiritual poisons is to allow the Holy Spirit to convict us. He will expose the buried garbage. The blood of Jesus cleanses us from sin first—then we need to allow the Holy Spirit to keep us clean. We have to choose not to take back the old ways, the old poisons. The Holy Spirit will not live in a pigpen! However, people have to be willing to not take back the bitterness, unforgiveness, and so on that will poison their spirits. They have to give up the old ways. Sadly, not many are willing to do that! And that is why there are so many sick among us. They *want,* but are unwilling to do what it takes to get. It is a choice. You cannot have your cake and eat it too. Let the Holy Spirit take control—yield to Him—then you will see good fruit. We cannot do this on our own strength. We need to allow the Holy Spirit to do it.

So as God exposes these leftovers, we need to be open to what He wants to do. You see God wants to heal us. He wants to do a work in us so that He can use us. But if we don't allow ourselves to admit these things and in addition if we try to "defend our position" arguing that we have a right to feel the way we do, it blocks God from doing His work in us. Then the leftovers are buried again and again, only to come out at a later time to torment us and put us back into a cycle of guilt and condemnation. We need to allow God to cleanse us and give us closure in these areas so we can be healed.

Sometimes our leftover is a "root vegetable." Just as a potato or carrot grows under the ground and can't be seen, our leftover is buried so deep that we don't realize it's there.

God will expose these roots. It is then when we need to pray and ask God to help us get rid of them. God wants us to be whole—physically, emotionally, and spiritually. It's a growth process that will continue as God refines us to be the person He created us to be. Refining is not to hurt us, but to take out the impurities so that we would be a holy people. And as this happens, others will see His light shine through us. God gave me an example of this to help me to understand better. He showed me a lamp that the light shone down from it, not up. Jesus shines His light down upon us. We are like reflectors. His light bounces and reflects off us for others to see. The cleaner the reflector, the more the light will shine from it. Then it was as if Jesus was polishing people's reflectors. I realized that this is what He did on the cross, and continues to do all the time for us. It is ongoing. He continues to "clean" us up as He exposes any cloudiness or film of sin on us. He exposes things in us that would never have gotten our attention before. He brings them to the surface so He can make us shinier and brighter. It's an ongoing process as He perfects us and brings us closer to Him. Then when we are in heaven with Him, we will be a bride without spot or wrinkle. So we shouldn't despise it when God shows us our shortcomings and failures, for as He deals with them, He does it in a loving way to bring us closer to Him. We should understand that when He brings these things to our attention, it's for our good, not to condemn. We must also remember that as we go through the fire and the leftovers are burned, that it is only the leftovers being burned—the flames will not harm us. Out of the fire comes pure gold.

As we grow and mature, we recognize our failures more easily. Sometimes it seems that we can't do anything right and we start to get discouraged. However, just the fact that we now recognize the failure, is a sign that we are learning. If we cannot recognize the failure, how can we learn from it? When we recognize what we've done and what we should have done instead, we learn how to handle the situation in a better way the next time. Failures help us to become all that God wants us to be if we learn from them. We start to recognize past experiences and learn to deal with them in the way God wants us to. It comes with experience, and experience comes many times by failing. How quick will we learn? If we don't learn the first time, we find the circumstance being repeated until we do learn. How many times does a baby fall before he learns to walk? The secret is in getting up. A boxer in the ring only loses when he doesn't get back up. When you fail, pick yourself up, dust yourself off and start all over again! (Wasn't there an old song that said that?)

Failures also are a reminder to us to be humble. We cannot do anything good in the flesh. When we fail, it keeps pride from coming in. We should not intentionally fail, but all fall short. It is a reminder to us that we can do nothing good without God. If we slip or fall, God is not ready to punish or condemn. We need to remember what Jesus did on the cross.

We need to look at the cross and not the failure. You see, letting the enemy put us under condemnation is the enemy's way of nullifying the cross. It's not that we can never fail, but the important thing is that we recognize it and ask forgiveness. As soon as we ask, we are forgiven. We do not have to ask forgiveness ten times or until we feel better to know we are forgiven. It is not your emotions that say whether you are forgiven or not. Faith is not how you feel. For as soon as you ask, you are forgiven. Don't let the enemy wear you down. Shine the cross in his face and watch him run! God has given us life and life more abundantly. (See John 10:10.) It is not a license to sin, but if we fail, we just need to come to Him. He is the way out of sin. He is the Way, the Truth, and the Life. He gives us everlasting life. Philippians 1:6 states, "Being confident of this very thing, that he which hath begun a good work in you will perform it until the day of Jesus Christ."

Chapter 3

Heaven's Door Is Open—
Won't You Come In?

$\mathcal{G}$ od wants everyone to spend eternity with Him in heaven. All are welcome. It doesn't matter who you are or what you've done. His mercy and grace are unending. He does not want any lost. (See John 17:12.)

Things of the Spirit are opposite from things of the flesh. The world says that if you confess your sin there is punishment. But Jesus says that once you confess your sin there is no remembrance of it. (See Hebrews 10:17.) You are washed clean and made new. And God sees us with new white garments, no spot or wrinkle. (See Ephesians 5:27.) In 1 John 1:9, it is written, "If we confess our sins He is faithful and just to forgive us our sins and to cleanse us from all unrighteousness."

It is so hard for us to understand this sometimes. It's not that we don't *know* it, it's that we find it hard to *believe* it.

As children we hide our mistakes from our parents for fear of punishment. But Jesus wants us to run to him with these things so we can be done with it and so that we can move on in our relationship with Him. The enemy makes this hard for us by tormenting us with fear, guilt, and condemnation. Jesus wants us to be free. In Romans 8:1, it states, "There is therefore now no condemnation to them which are in Christ Jesus." But we think in human terms and experiences. Parents sometimes will deny their children's bad behavior, even saying, "My child can do no wrong." This teaches the child to cover up his sins and not to confess them to Jesus. On the other hand, some parents are so ready to punish that the child is afraid to confess his sins to Jesus, thinking that his heavenly Father is harsh.

How it must grieve God, who is Love, to see us going through agony emotionally when we sin because others punish us with grudges, or not forgiving us right away, or forgiving us with "buts," or bringing up past issues and not forgetting them. We carry these belief systems into adulthood, making us bound. Yes, discipline with love is necessary in the world, but we must realize that once we confess our sins, God sees His children through the blood of Jesus as righteous. He wants us free. He wants us to walk in His righteousness.

So often, God teaches me by example. One day I had a vision of Jesus and me walking hand in hand along a path. It seemed as if it was a heavenly area. He told me that He was leading me on the path of righteousness. As we walked, I could see my old dirty clothes falling to the ground piece by piece and a new white garment being placed on me. He was showing me that as I walk with Him, I have His righteousness. There is no room for guilt and condemnation. I felt that He was saying that my righteousness is of Him and that I should never forget it.

As we learn and grow in Him, we see in our hearts as well
as in our minds, what Jesus accomplished on the cross. It's
then that we acknowledge and receive what He did for us.
When we do this it pleases Him. How would we feel if we
suffered on the cross for someone else's sins and they didn't
receive that gift? We would feel as if we did it for nothing.
As we grow, we learn not to accept the devil's lies, especially when he tries to put guilt and condemnation in. We
become more confident in this knowledge. I am not refer-
ring to "head" knowledge like in a history book, but heart
knowledge. It's when we understand this in our hearts that
we have freedom.

After a failure, we sometimes let the enemy toy with our
emotions and put guilt, sadness, depression and whatever else
he would put in our minds that will make us feel miserable.
But God's love for us has nothing to do with how we feel!
God's love is always there for us! We may think that He's not
there because our emotions block us from feeling His presence. One day, as I was feeling sad, God asked me if my feelings were more important than His Word and His promises?
I realized then that my emotions had taken over to the point
where I was dwelling on them rather than what God's Word
said. When God's Word says we are forgiven, why would we
dwell on our mistakes? When we keep mulling over our failures and keep letting the enemy put thoughts of unworthiness
in us, we are not giving God the glory for what Jesus did on
the cross for us!

When will we learn to break out of that mold? It must be
so frustrating to Jesus to see us suffer, especially when He took
all that upon Himself on the cross and suffered in our place.
It must grieve Him to see us go through needless torment as
we hide from Him instead of running to Him to receive His

forgiveness, love, and comfort. His arms are always open—no matter what!

Some of you may say, "But my faith is not strong enough!" Others may think that you need to be perfect for God to love you. I believe that God wants His people to know that perfection, just as beauty, is in the eye of the beholder. No one is perfect, but even if that were so, if God only cared about the perfect, what hope would that be for others? We need to know that through the blood of Jesus, we are made perfect in His sight. We do not and cannot walk in our own perfection, but in His. Weakness isn't necessarily a bad thing as long as we acknowledge it. It keeps us humble. Then we will depend on God. God wants us to walk in His strength, not ours!

In Romans 7:15, Paul is talking about how he doesn't understand himself at all. He is saying that he does things he doesn't want to do and that the Spirit is at war with the flesh. We struggle with this every day. Paul says that his new life tells him to do what's right, but his old nature still loves to sin. He goes on to ask who will free him from his slavery to his old nature? He answers by saying it has been done by Jesus—He has set him free.

We should never give up! We need to keep running the race as Paul states in 1 Corinthians 9:24. As we fight these battles, we grow stronger, and after each battle comes a victory that brings us closer to God. Then we become stronger, purer, and rid of another stronghold that would keep us bound. All we need to do is confess our sin and repent of it. After the Israelites won their battles, they received the spoils. As we do spiritual battles to overcome our struggles, we also receive the spoils (blessings).

We need to understand that there is nothing we can do to make God stop loving us! Jesus gave His life for us! No one can fully understand doing this unless they have done it. However we can understand this—that since God loved us enough to send Jesus to die for us, He also loves us enough to never leave us and to always love us. In Isaiah 49:15, it states that even if a mother could forget her child, God will not forget you. Sometimes when we fall, we feel like failures. However we need to remind ourselves that God doesn't make failures. I think it saddens Him when we feel that way. And even when we fall, He's always there to catch us, holding our hand. Psalm 37:24 reminds us that though he fall, he won't be cast down.

I remember hearing one pastor say that being justified means that when we confess our sins, it's "just if I'd" never sinned. What a great way to see it!

We must learn to keep ourselves open and exposed before God. We need to keep short accounts. We already have the answer—take it to the cross right away and then leave it there! Otherwise that sin becomes a link in a chain—a piece of wall between you and God. The more links, the longer the chain so that after a while the enemy has you dragging a ball and chain, and it becomes heavier and heavier as you become bound.

It is so unnecessary, as Jesus has already given us freedom. If only we would come to Him and expose the sin. That's how we walk in freedom—freedom from sickness, emotional problems, or whatever else has us bound—that is how we obtain deliverance. Keep yourselves transparent before the Lord, and then darkness cannot come in. You see, if the enemy knows that every time he comes at you with condemnation you run to Jesus and draw close to Him, he will give up. Darkness cannot remain dark when it is exposed to light. That is why the enemy has to work by deceit. Once he's exposed, he has no power!

One of my favorite movies when I was a child was *The Wizard of Oz*. Dorothy and all the munchkins were afraid of the wizard. But when Dorothy actually saw the wizard, he was a little man with no power, just devices to make him seem powerful. The enemy is just like that. He uses devices to make us afraid.

God wants us to have life abundantly. He freely gives it to us. But we separate ourselves from Him by holding onto our "little" sins like they were treasures to keep in a secret place. If only God's people would clean house. They would have freedom such as they've never known. Just come to God and give Him all these things and you will feel lighter, the burdens lifted, the junk cleaned out. Then after you have given it to God, *believe* that God has forgiven you and then *forgive yourselves!* When Jesus died on the cross, He said, "It is finished". Leave it there. Don't hold onto it. Don't take it back. Confess, repent, and let it go. It is finished. God's Word states in Hebrews 8:12 that He will remember our sins no more. If He can forget them, why can't we?

In these last days, the enemy will be attacking more and more. But if you know these things, he cannot harm you. You will not be defeated! His fiery darts will be like an air gun—harmless! Guilt and condemnation will have no place in you—freedom will abound. Jesus died on the cross for you. Don't you see that you were worthy enough in His sight for Him to do that for you? Understand this and then you will realize the impact of the Scripture, "There is now no condemnation for those in Christ Jesus". Let it sink into your very being. Then the enemy's darts will have no impact. You can always come to Jesus knowing that nothing can separate you from His love. Do not let the enemy put walls up between you and Jesus. Always come before Him with everything.

Then the only walls that can go up are walls of imagination put there in your mind from the enemy.

You see, it's *what* you do when you fail that matters, not the failure. God knew we would fail at times. In Psalm 139, God told us that He knew what we were going to say and do even before we were formed. So, it's not the fact that we failed—people dwell on the failure—they should instead dwell on the cross and what *Jesus* did, not what they did! Humble yourself, repent, and be thankful for what Jesus did and then move on! Failures certainly keep us humble, for if we think that we do everything right, that's when we get "puffed up." When we fail, we should not feel guilty or condemned, but rather recognize our need of Jesus and what He did for us. Our righteousness is of Him. For the humble are lifted up, but the proud are brought down. God's greatest servants in the Bible were those who saw their frailties and knew their need of Him. They were humble, yet they were great in God's eyes. The danger lies, not in the failure itself, because when we see the failure we can come to the cross and ask forgiveness. It seems to me that the greater danger is in not recognizing the sin. Those in danger are the ones who don't think they sin and go around blinded to it. They see themselves as perfect, but they are imperfect. The ones that see themselves as being imperfect are perfected in Jesus.

Things of the Spirit are opposite things of the flesh. So when we sin, we should be thankful that we recognize it and therefore can ask forgiveness and repent. Perception can be deception when we look at things through the eyes of the flesh. Perception can be conception when we see how God looks at us, through the blood of Jesus. We conceive what His promises are for us, and then we can receive them.

If we learn from the failure, it is growth. We are being

perfected with each failure—for most times, we don't learn from what we do right, but from our mistakes. So even by learning from our failures, God works all things for good. There is no growth without change, and there is no change without learning from our mistakes. It is a learning process. The enemy would have you live in condemnation. That is the opposite of what Jesus did. It's so easy for people to believe the enemy's lies because the world punishes. But Jesus forgives right away. Just ask and it's done.

We sometimes have such difficulty believing we've failed. We ask ourselves, how could we have messed up? We should remember that we are being made perfect, but perfection will not come until we are in heaven. When we get so upset with ourselves and won't let it go, even after asking for forgiveness, we need to realize that it's actually pride coming in to make us think we were too good to have sinned in the first place. Then we get discouraged. All we need to do is ask forgiveness and then immediately pick ourselves up, dust ourselves off and move on. The fact that we recognize our sin and know to ask forgiveness right away is a step in the right direction. Jesus died for our sins because He knew we weren't perfect. Let's give Him glory for what He's done and then try, try again.

God created everything. He made the trees, flowers, birds, fish, sun, moon, and stars—the earth and all that is within. However, Jesus didn't die on the cross for those things that God created. He died for *us*. He enjoys the beauty of these other things, but He loves *us*. When we receive Him, we are one with Him. It's just the opposite of a natural birth. When we are born, we become separate from our mothers. Yet when we are born again, we become one with God—just the opposite. He gave us the birds, the fish, the trees, and all these things to enjoy just as He enjoys them. He created all, but He loves us.

God wants to bless His children more than we could ever know. He wants us to have knowledge about these things so that we will not have walls up—so that we can be closer to Him and receive all that He has for us. He wants us to know these things so that we can believe Him for all that He wants to do in our lives. For how can we believe that He wants to bless *us* if we're under guilt and condemnation? He wants us to walk in the freedom of all that He has for us. We think our failures separate us from God. However, they only can do this if we don't give them to Jesus. When we come to Him with our failures, they actually draw us closer to Him as we learn more and more about His love and forgiveness for us. We learn about His mercy and grace. In this way God even turns our failures for our good.

It makes God happy when we know that He loves us and will bless us in spite of our failures. It makes Him happy when we expect Him to be loving and kind to us, even when we mess up. And as we learn about God's love for us, we can trust Him more. It pleases God when we finally understand how much He loves us—and then realize that nothing can separate us from Him, and nothing can change His plans to bless us, if we come to Him right away when we fail.

God wants us to know that no matter how many times we fail, Jesus still forgives us. All it takes is for us to come to Him and say we're sorry, and He forgives. We don't want to fail—we just do. Satan would have you think, well, I did this again! This is it! I can't be forgiven again. It's a lie. Then discouragement comes in, then condemnation from the enemy. Then we fear coming to Jesus. It becomes like a strap around your chest, being tightened by the enemy, to squeeze the life out. Don't fall for it!

Some people take longer than others to overcome. Jesus

is love. And Scripture tells us that love is patient, love is kind, love never notices when others do things wrong. We are constantly under construction, learning to trust God in our failures and learning to forgive others when they fail us. We are running the race waiting to get the prize, which is when we are made to perfection when we are in heaven. Until that time, we need to persevere. The only way we can be defeated is if we give up on ourselves. Jesus will never give up on us.

In addition to looking to the cross, we need also to look at the empty tomb. The empty tomb represents life—after the cross, we are reborn. The tomb is God's promises fulfilled. Death is conquered, and we have eternal life. The cross is where sins were forgiven; the empty tomb is where new life is given. We have to die to our sins and nail them to the cross. Then we are given a new life, which is of the Spirit. This is what "born of the Spirit" means. When people die, their bodies are an empty tomb. Their spirit is resurrected.

Life on earth is to prepare us for life eternal in heaven. As a baby, we need to learn basic things like walking and talking. A baby's world is himself. Then as a child, we learn behavioral skills for getting along with others in this world. But we still see ourselves as the center. Then, as we start to mature and start to grow spiritually, we see ourselves becoming smaller and smaller as we yield to God, so that eventually the center of our world is God, and not ourselves.

In this world, being independent is a virtue. Spiritually, giving up your independence and becoming dependent on God is a virtue. Things of the Spirit are opposite things of the flesh. That's why it's so hard for people to give God control over their lives. Since childhood, they are taught to be independent, to take care of themselves, which is necessary in the natural. Spiritually, it's a whole different concept—totally opposite of what the world teaches—to be completely dependent on God. They have to learn to trust Him for the answers and not their human reasoning. They have to learn to come to God right away with a problem, instead of trying to "fix" it themselves first. People consider themselves successful if they know all the answers, if they know how to handle everything on their own. God considers them successful when they look to Him first. (See Isaiah 55:8–9.)

It's humbling for people to understand that they do not know the best way to handle everything. Pride gets in the way. But you see, the Creator knows the beginning and the end; people don't. People could save themselves a lot of time and trouble by just *asking* God. Even with the "little" things. We sometimes don't want to bother Him with everything, but that's exactly what He wants. He wants to be a part of every area of our lives. We have to retrain ourselves to give it all to God—every little thing, not just the big things. Most of the time we don't even think to give it to God, so we try to make everything work ourselves. Then when it gets so messed up we can't handle it, we give God our mess. If we will give things to God when they are small, we will be amazed how smoothly everything works out. That's the secret. That's when we will grow and mature. We need to trust God that His plans for us are better than our plans for us. (See Jeremiah 29:11.)

The Christian life is a battle between the flesh and the spirit. But with each battle, as we learn to die to flesh and be controlled by our spirit, it prepares us and brings us closer to heaven. These battles are not futile—it's necessary to crucify the flesh. We grow in the Spirit with each victory. At first, the flesh is bigger than the spirit. But each time flesh is denied, it gets smaller and your spirit gets bigger. Until at last the Spirit rules and not the flesh. Then we walk in the Spirit and not the flesh. This is how we are being perfected as we go through life. As previously stated, a baby's world is himself, his flesh. Then he learns to share, to deny himself of something he wants. And so the process begins of learning to deny the flesh and feed the spirit. Maturity is when the spirit has grown so much that we see the world in terms of others, not ourselves.

Life is a process of perfecting that which will come to God. We are all a work in progress. God gave me an example of this by showing me how a caterpillar turns into a butterfly. That's what happens when we become born-again. We become a new creation, a different person. What we did in the past, who we were, died with the old creature, the caterpillar. It is dead, buried and forgotten. The new creation has nothing to do with the past. It is totally different. Like the caterpillar that is now a butterfly, we are transformed spiritually into a different person. Johnny caterpillar is dead— Johnny butterfly is not the same. Butterflies are free—they fly. When you are born again you are free; you can soar to new levels in Christ. Then we understand that during those times when we don't do or say the right things, God still loves us. We understand this at these times of failure even more than when we do everything right. It's also during those times, when we learn to love others more, despite their failures. We are learning that love never notices when others do things wrong. (See 1 Corinthians 13:4.) So if we, as flesh and blood, can love others when they fall short, how much more does our Father still love us. It is because of those times that we learn to be more like Jesus.

As we are growing, we are learning to recognize when we

slip and fall right away, and to come to Jesus and confess it right away. We are learning to be transparent and not let the enemy put a wedge in between God and ourselves. We learn from our mistakes, not our perfections. So therefore we should not despise our mistakes, for they are what helps us grow. God turns all things for good.

Chapter 4

Intimacy

God wants intimacy with us. But in order for us to be intimate with God, we have to bare our soul. We have to let God know everything about us—the good, the bad, and the ugly. He already knows, but by the act of us telling Him ourselves, it shows Him that we trust Him enough to love us in spite of our faults and weaknesses. It shows God that we trust Him to never leave us or forsake us, no matter what. And this is pleasing to God. Only then can there be no walls between you and God, and there's true intimacy. We fellowship with friends, yet most friends don't know the intimate details of our soul. Even in some marriages, there is only physical intimacy, which is not complete intimacy. God wants true intimacy so that He can abide in us and we can abide in Him.

We also need to know God more, so that we can be intimate

with Him. But how do we get to know God more? One way is by asking Him questions about how He feels about certain issues. He will let us see His heart if we ask Him.

Suppose God were in a boat with us, each of us with an oar, rowing right alongside the other. What would happen if we were the only one rowing? With one oar, we would just go in circles. We would not have any idea of God's direction in our lives. God wants to be a part of our lives. He wants us to come to Him and share with Him our hopes and dreams, our joys and needs. He wants us to ask Him about His desires for us. He wants us to talk with Him as we would a daddy, or our husband or friend. That is His desire—to have communion with us. He wants to nurture us. Our prayers do not have to be long or complicated, just from our hearts. He wants friendship and intimacy, not formality. He wants us to talk to Him as a friend. Then as you know God's heart for you, you will have more intimacy with Him. It will also affect your heart when you know how God feels. God wants His people to know Him. It breaks His heart when the only way people know Him is through what their traditions tell them. He wants them to know His heart, to know His love, to feel what He's feeling. God loves to have fellowship with His children, but intimacy is greater. It's more than fellowship. Fellowship is for friends; intimacy is for lovers. God is the Lover of our souls. He says, "Be Mine." God wants us to rest in Him. He showed me that a bed is a place of rest and comfort, and of intimacy. It's a place where we are exposed. It's a place where innermost secrets are told without fear of rejection—a place where you are loved just the way you are. God is that place of rest where we can be naked before Him and know that He loves us just the way we are.

As I was telling God how much I needed Him, He let me know that He needs us, too. God owns everything. There is not one thing He lacks. But everyone needs love, even God. He needs us to love Him and to communicate with Him. We sometimes forget that God has feelings too. He made us in His image. But since He is God, He loves more. Just as we need to be with and talk to our spouses and to know their love, so does God want to be with us and talk to us and to know our love for Him. God created every-thing—the birds, flowers—all that is in the earth. He cre-ated them for us to enjoy just as He enjoys them. But He created Adam and Eve for love. He created all, but He loves us and needs our love, too!

Sometimes we get so busy learning *about* God that we do not take the time to *be with* God. Teaching and learning are both good, but all work and all busyness are not good. If we were to talk about business or daily routine with our spouses all the time, it would leave no room for intimacy. Would the spark of romance be kept alive? Would we feel that closeness that only lovers can have? God needs that intimacy with us too. We also need that intimacy with Him. Otherwise we feel empty. Teach-ing is the food to help you grow, but intimacy is the dessert!

One day God gave me a picture of synchronized swimming. He showed me how everyone moves the same way at the same time—like poetry in motion. That's what it's like when we walk "in the Spirit." Our spirits are in tune with God's Spirit. Every-thing works perfectly. When a part of our natural body is "out of sync," nothing works right. When our spirit is out of sync with God's Spirit, nothing goes right. We need to stay in sync with God. We do this by prayer and communication with Him. The trouble is many of us do not want to make the effort, or we are so busy and tired, we cannot. How do we do this in this age of no time? I questioned this myself on days when I needed an extra twenty-four hours to get things done. The answer comes in training ourselves to think of God often and talk to Him as we go about our daily routine. So much of our thoughts are escape thoughts to get our minds off all we have to do and our daily stresses. But God wants us to escape to Him. He is our refuge and our strength. He will give us rest and peace.

God's presence is always with us. When we receive Him, we are one with Him. We are born again. It is just the opposite of a natural birth. When we are born naturally, we become separate from our mother. Yet with the new birth, we become one with God. He is in us, we in Him. We can never be separated. Something that is one cannot be separated. Each part has some of the other in it. Even when we feel like God is not with us, He is. The only difference between when we feel His presence and when we do not is that our attention is not on Him because we have other things on our minds. It does not mean that God is not there with us. It's just that we are focused on other things. We usually feel God's presence in our prayer time. That is because we have taken the time to be with Him, and our focus is on Him. It's all on our end, because God's focus is always on us.

After Jesus' resurrection, He was walking with the disciples, yet they did not know it was Him. He was with them even when they didn't realize it! Just because our minds might be on other things doesn't mean He is not there. We can talk to Him at all times. All we have to do is turn our thoughts to Him. He is part of us, and we are part of Him. If we drink a glass of water, the water is in us. It becomes a part of us, and we become a part of it. It is integrated. We are integrated with God. He is always part of us, never separate. Once people realize this so that they know it in their hearts, they will not fear. It states in Matthew 28:20, "And, lo, I am with you always, even unto the end of the world."

One of Satan's strategies is to get you to fear because you think that God is not with you. That is why it is so important to come to God right away when sin or troubles come. Then Satan cannot put discouragement or despair in your mind. All we need to do is come to God and then use God's sword (His Word) against the enemy. (See Romans 8:38–39.) True intimacy is having the freedom to know that you can call on God and talk to Him about anything, and God will not be angry with you or stop loving you. God will never hang up on you. We can always trust in His loving kindness to us.

When we realize that we can come to Him with anything, the bad as well as the good, and He will listen, it pleases Him. I believe that sometimes when we are in our weakest of moments, we discover that those times can also be our most intimate moments with God. We can speak frankly to God about the way we feel. To just come to God only when we are strong, to always pretend to feel joy and say the same things, is robotic. But when we speak what we feel, we are passionate about it. We can be passionate with joy, or passionate with discouragement, but having passion about something is speaking from our heart. It is our heart's cry to God, and when our heart speaks, God listens. That is how breakthrough comes. Intimacy is heart to heart. Intimacy is when we share our joys as well as our sorrows with God. He gives us His permission to do it. God wants all of us, not just the happy side. We should not close off the discouragement side for fear of God being upset with us. He wants us to reveal all of our heart to Him. It's then that we will see greater intimacy with Him.

As we are intimate with God, we come alive. God is life. We have energy, joy, and abundant life. Who could ask for anything more?

Chapter 5

God's Power:
The Battery Charger of Life

*G*od has planted seeds of faith in us. When we water them, they will grow. But how do we water them? It is with God's Word. God's Word is the very strongest thing we can have. He has planted His words in our hearts, the core of our being. His Word always produces fruit. It is power. It is the secret to victory. Most people know it, but they don't use God's Word. Or if they do, it is not used as much as it should be used. That is why there is weakness. They only plant one seed (word), when God has given them many. There is power in His Word, for it is life. We need to read it, plant it in our hearts, and then speak it (sow it) until we see the fruit.

People's faith is increased when they see signs and wonders following God's Word. They see the reality of it. However, people who have not witnessed the reality of God's Word by seeing signs and wonders, have trouble believing it. They think that God *can* heal, but they don't know that God *will* heal because they have not witnessed it. As a result, their faith is weak. They go through the motions of praying because they think that *maybe* it will work. They hope, but cannot believe that God will answer as *fact*. An example is how people look at what God's Word says about money. In Malachi, God says to test Him with our tithes and offerings. God does not need our money. He says this because people need to see the results, the harvest of it. People have a hard time with money. (If you knew I was going to mention this, would you have started to read this chapter?) Some people put a little in the offering plate because that is what they have always done. But they were never taught the reality of God's Word. Tithing is the biggest hurdle to get over. In some churches it is never talked about. That may be because of fear that membership may drop. That is why God says to test Him in this area. When people understand this and see what happens, they won't stop tithing. In fact they are ready, anxious and excited to give knowing that God always gives back more. God never meant for Christians to live in poverty. He has shown them the way, so why won't they obey? For some, it is lack of knowledge; they were never told. For others, it is love of money. Yet for others, it is their lack of faith in believing God's Word. God has so much for us! Why can't we take Him at His Word? Psalm 37:3 states, "Trust in the Lord, and do good; so shalt thou dwell in the land, and verily thou shalt be fed."

We always seem to accept things in the natural much easier than we accept things in the supernatural. Water in a river always runs downstream. It does not go upstream. If we drop a rock, it will fall to the ground. When a balloon is filled with helium, it floats up. The sun always rises in the east. These are natural laws. We believe them because we see them. However there are also supernatural laws. When we give, we will receive—this is so, whether it's money or a smile. When you pray, God hears and answers. These are spiritual laws. They cannot be changed. We should believe them just as we do the natural laws. That is when we have spiritual sight. We see and understand these things just as we see the natural. When we walk in the natural, we see in the natural. When we walk in the Spirit, we see the supernatural.

We believe, and our faith is increased when we see the reality of God's Word. He knows we are but dust. That's why Jesus did signs and wonders as He walked the earth. That's why He gave us authority to so the same in His name. God's power in churches is life.

People sometimes make it so hard for God to give to them. It's as if they don't want to receive God's gifts. God has so much for His people, yet they block Him from giving to them! One way that they block receiving what God has for them is by unbelief. They cannot believe God wants to bless them. This is possibly because of hidden, past or unconfessed sin in their lives. Or people sometimes feel, whether consciously or subconsciously, that it is a sign of weakness or charity to be given something that they didn't work for. They transfer this feeling from the natural to the spiritual. They have trouble understanding the spiritual. They have trouble believing what God has for them. They go by what their senses tell them in the natural. They mix up the flesh with spiritual and see it as weakness. It's pride that they didn't do it themselves. But even the special talents and abilities we have doesn't come from us, they come from God. We need to realize that if we do our job well, it's God that gave us that ability and to give Him glory. These are some things of the flesh that prevent blessings.

49

God says in His Word, "Beloved, I wish above all things that thou mayest prosper and be in health, even as thy soul prospereth" (3 John 1:2). God desires to give us good gifts. I thought of the old motivational saying, if you can dream it, you can have it. That depends entirely on our own abilities. Yet things of the Spirit are opposite things of the flesh. The flesh says "I'll believe it when I receive it." The Spirit says, "I believe God's Word, therefore I will receive it." (See Matthew 21:22.) This means that receiving God's blessings has nothing to do with our efforts; it is God's goodness. All we have to do is take Him at His Word. What God says He will do, He will do!

Christians are being oppressed, depressed, living in sickness and poverty. That is not God's will for them. He has given us His Word. All we need to do is believe and obey. In Psalm 81:10, God tells us to open our mouths wide and see if He won't fill it. He asks us to come to Him and trust Him. As a baby bird opens its mouth and its mother fills it, God says He will fill ours. The mouth is where our bodies are sustained. It is where we take in food and water, what we need for life. God says to open our mouths *wide* so that He can give us everything we need. In fact, He gives us even more and that's why it says to open our mouths wide! Yet, people will not receive what God has for them; instead they receive from the enemy. They believe what the enemy tells them and not God's Word.

To receive healing and provision, we need to believe that God wants to bless *us*. Just as we earthly parents are happy to give our children gifts, it gives God joy to give good gifts to us. When we ask according to God's will for us, we need to believe that He wants to give it to us, and receive it. If your child asked you for an increase in his allowance so that he could give to the poor, wouldn't you grant it? We would be happy that he wanted to give. So we don't need to wonder if God will grant our request if it is according to His will for us. We just need to know His will, and believe that when we ask, we will receive. We need to expect it. God is a good Daddy. He wants the very best for His children. When we don't allow ourselves to receive from God, we deny God the pleasure of giving to us. In the natural, it gives us pleasure to give to those in need. In the spiritual, it gives God pleasure to give to us, because He loves us and we love Him and want to obey Him. That is all He asks of us. Yet we feel unworthy to receive, because we know we fall short.

Thank God, Jesus has taken care of it! When we fail, and we do because we are not perfect, we should not let the enemy put in guilt in and tell us that we can't be blessed. That is a lie. It's so much easier for us to believe that God will forgive us than it is to believe that God will bless us. God is always ready to forgive and to give. The enemy would tell you otherwise so that you don't expect blessings. If you don't expect them, you will not look to receive them. That is how Satan robs us. He convinces us in our minds that we sinned, so we should give up and not expect God to still bless us. But God still forgives and still gives. God does not withhold blessings because of performance. (See Romans 7:15–25.)

He blesses us because we're His children, and He loves us. He sees our heart and knows that we don't want to fail. But as we ask forgiveness and then trust Him to forgive us and love us enough to bless us anyway just *because* He loves us, it pleases Him. It is not because of our goodness that He blesses us, but because of *His* goodness. If we can believe God's goodness for salvation, and forgiveness of sins when we fail, then we can believe in His goodness to bless us too. His goodness isn't partial or limited. He does not have goodness for one thing and not the other. He is not man for which that may be true. He is Love. He is Goodness. Surely goodness and mercy shall follow you all the days of your life. (See Psalm 23:6.)

Sometimes the enemy will lie to us and he will tell us to be complacent and "accept our lot" in life. How it must hurt God's feelings for us to say, "No thank you, I'm happy with what I have," when He wants to give us more! I think that people misinterpret the scripture where Paul says he is content in whatever state he is in. I don't think that means that we shouldn't ask God to meet our needs or that we shouldn't believe Him for all He has for us. I understand it to mean that when we are going through a trial, we should be at peace knowing that God will deliver us and take care of us. God showed me the word *contentment* broken up into the prefix *con*, meaning "with" (Latin) and *tent*, meaning "covering." He showed me that when we are contented, we know that in all things, at all times, no matter what we're going through, God is with us and He is our covering, our shelter. His hand covers us (blessings); His blood covers us (healing, protection and deliverance.) That is contentment. It means we have peace, knowing that God is in control.

I believe God always wants more for His children, just as we want more for ours. We need to have our spiritual ears and eyes open to hear and see God's plans for us. It's a lie of the enemy (to keep God's people in poverty) to think that prosperity is not godly. He tries to make us think that money is bad. But he is a master at twisting words, for the Bible says that it's the *love* of money that is evil, not the money. (See 1 Timothy 6:10.) As long as we give to others, keep our eyes on the Lord, stay humble, and not put value on things, then blessings will be given to us. One problem arises when God blesses us, if we take the credit and think that we did it by our own efforts. We need to give God the glory, for He gives us every good and perfect gift. Also, it's when we desire these things more than God, and put more importance on them than God that is wrong. Those who desire things above God will not have them. If we put God first, if He and His kingdom purposes are most important to us, then God will prosper us so that we can use what He gives us for His glory. (See Matthew 6:33.) Then as we give, He gives us more so that we can give more, and so on. It's God's will for us to prosper. As I stated before, 3 John 1:2 says, "Beloved, I wish above all things that thou mayest prosper and be in health, even as thy soul prospereth." When he says He wishes above *all* things, could there be any question that God wants to bless us? How can we help others in need or put back into God's kingdom if we're all poor? We should never let the enemy make us feel guilty for receiving the blessings God gives to us.

Yet you ask, how do people who don't have much to give walk in God's provision and health? God doesn't require much. If you have a loaf of bread, give a slice. If you are sick, pray for others who are sick. God doesn't ask you to give what you don't have. Even the widow woman only had enough for one cake, yet she gave to Elijah. The widow woman in the temple got Jesus' attention when she gave only a few pennies. Yet her giving meant more than the rich people's gifts, for she gave all she had. (See Mark 12:42–44.) This scripture shows us that our giving is proportionate to what we have: "Give, and it shall be given unto you; good measure, pressed down, and shaken together, and running over, shall men give into your bosom" (Luke 6:38).

Faith *comes* by hearing, and hearing by the Word of God. But faith is *increased* by taking action on the Word and then by our seeing the results. When you hear the Word, you have faith to believe. When you *obey* the Word, you have the answers. When we hear the scripture that I mentioned above, "Give and it shall be given unto you," we have faith and we believe that if we give, it will be given unto us. But when we actually take action and obey the word and give, then we will receive and see the Word work in our lives. Then our faith will increase.

Sometimes God will open doors to bless us. Many times we will start to go through them, but when it comes down to really taking action and doing it in faith, the enemy starts to put doubts and excuses in us as to why we can't do it. It's true, we cannot do it, but if God opens the door, what seems impossible to man, is not to God. However as we just obey God and step out in faith—that's when we see miracles! You see, it takes a miracle from God to do something we know we cannot! That is why on occasion God will tell us to do what seems impossible to us, to test our faith to see if even though we know it can't be done in the natural, we'll take action and believe anyway.

There is no need for a miracle to happen if we can take care of it ourselves. Do you have faith enough to believe? It is always our own choice whether or not to walk through the door. I knew a person who wasn't walking in all that God had for him. Whenever God would open a door of opportunity for this person, he would take the first step but then would not follow up and take the next one. He would procrastinate for so long that the opportunity would pass by. There was always a "good excuse" not to do it. God has so much more for this person than they will allow themselves to receive.

The saying, "you can lead a horse to water but you can't make him drink" is very true. Those that are looking for God's

plans to be worked out in their lives, will allow God to prepare their hearts and increase their faith to choose to walk
through the door and receive all that He has for them.

God wants to know, how badly do you want it? Can you
believe for the impossible? I remember a case my husband had
concerning a youth that was incarcerated. This youth wanted
to leave the country to go on a mission trip. By human reasoning, it seemed impossible, but the Holy Spirit told my
husband what to do. He stepped out in faith and saw God
do miracles. The youth was given a furlough from prison and
was allowed to go. We believe miracles can happen to others.
Why don't we apply the same faith when it comes to personal
instruction from God?

We need to seize the moment! Timing is everything. Maybe
God has given you instruction and He is now waiting to see
your faith. Maybe you keep waiting for more, when God has
already done what He's going to do and now it's up to you to
do your part. What good is an open door if you don't walk
through it?

God has so much for us. We need to stop "fighting" it with
reasons why it can't work and start walking into our blessings.

You may feel that your need is too small to bother God
with. But God cares about the little things too. His Word says
that even the hairs on your head are numbered. (See Luke
12:7.) That Word shows us that He cares for every little detail
about us. He wants us to look to Him in faith knowing that
He will handle the small things as well. If our child came
running to us with a scratch on his knee, would we say to
him, "It's only a scratch. Fix it by yourself. Come back if it's
broken?" Yet some people trust God for one thing and not the
other. They believe Him for this problem and not the other
one. God is not a God of partiality! We need to trust Him in

the small things, as well as the large. We should not rob God of His pleasure in helping us, and not rob Him of His glory when we see the answers. God wants us to trust Him in our time of trouble so that He can rescue us and we can give Him glory. (See Psalm 50:15.)

You may feel afraid. What if you fail? But if God told you to do it, then do not worry about giving yourself credit for failing. You may feel subconsciously that you don't deserve it—you're right, you don't! But God wants to give it to you anyway. Jesus died on the cross for us. If we were perfect, He would not have had to do it.

God will tell us to do things that seem so contrary to our thinking, so impossible, but that's so when it actually comes about we know it is God who has done it. There's no question, and we can take no credit. To God be the glory! We need to be careful that we don't let the enemy rob us of what God wants for us by believing him when he tells us it won't work. The only way we can be sure it won't work is if we don't do it! I can't imagine how frustrating it is for God to have such blessings for us and then to watch us let them pass us by. God has purposed us all for something special. How we can miss the mark!

God gave me a message that I will never forget about faith. He showed me that He had a huge box. Then He showed me that I had a small box. His box had so many good things inside for me, but He told me that He could not fit a huge box inside of a small one. It's not possible. He told me that I needed to expand my faith to believe so that I could receive all that He wants to give me. He's just waiting so that our box will be big enough to receive what's in His box. God always confirms what He tells us. About six weeks later I was reading the book, *The Prayer of Jabez*. There was a story in it about boxes of blessings that God had in heaven that were never opened. It really caught my attention. We can't fathom all the blessings that God has for us.

I sometimes wonder if God allows us to go through trials simply because we're not listening and walking in what He has for us. Maybe He needs to get our attention, so that He can bless us and we won't miss out on what He has for us. Sometimes we get stagnant. Stagnation is when people get so comfortable where they are at, they don't want change in their lives. If everything is going pretty well, they're afraid of change. When this happens, there is no expectancy.

How can God do miracles when people don't even think to look for them? It is easy to get complacent and comfortable, never moving forward, not even moving backward! It is comfortable to become neither hot nor cold. But you see, without change, there is no growth. Without change, God cannot do all the good He has for us. If only people would step out in faith and allow God to work change in their lives. There's so much more He would do for them, if only they could believe.

There are three things that stand in people's way. The first is a lack of trust. They have to trust God enough to give Him control. They have to trust Him enough to know that He has better things for them than they have for themselves.

The second thing is that they limit God. They see Him according to their natural senses. They think of God in terms of what man can do, not who He is. Man has still not comprehended the vastness of the universe, yet God made it. He is larger than the universe, yet man does not see Him as limitless. They limit Him by their faith, for God will only do what their faith allows them to believe for. God wants so much to bless His people, yet they limit Him with their senses. We need to expand our faith, to dare to believe. We have no trouble believing that a good friend will do something that we've asked him to do for us. The reason that we trust he will do it is because we gave him something that we know he is capable of doing. It is harder for people to believe God, because they ask for things that are, in their minds, humanly impossible. But God is the God of impossibilities! God's Word says, in Jeremiah 32:17, that "there is nothing too hard for God." People think of God in human terms. However what's impossible for us is possible with God! In John 14:11–14, it says to believe Him for the very works that He does. It then goes on to say that whatever we ask in Jesus' name, it shall be done. If we can believe that a friend will do what we ask, and he or she is only human, how much more can we believe God? How much more can God be trusted to do it?

The biggest stumbling block for people is that they think of God as human—and what they can do. They think in terms of their own human reasoning and understanding. They box God in with human limitations. Let God out of the box and see what He won't do for you! Understand that He is God. Yet He can only do for people what they can believe Him for. Prayer and faith are the fuel that can move mountains. In Matthew 17:20, we are told that even if we have faith as small as a grain of mustard seed, we can say to this mountain, "move," and it shall. Jesus couldn't do as many miracles as He wanted to do in His own town because the people didn't believe that He could. They said that He was just like them, born here in this town. They thought of Him in human terms.

The third thing is that people have trouble believing for themselves. They believe that God will bless others, but not them. This is most likely because they know what they've done, so they reason that God will not bless them. But God forgives and forgets. We may not forget all we've done wrong. But God does. As I was thinking about people feeling that they do not deserve God's blessings, I felt like God was asking me, "Is that why you give to your children, because they deserve it? Because they are perfect at all times?" Of course not!

How much more does God love His children and want to give to them! It has nothing to do with deserving anything. That's one of the lies of the enemy that people believe most, that God won't bless them because they don't deserve it. And they believe the enemy because they *know* that they don't deserve it. The enemy speaks to us in the same way that he twisted things to Eve in the Garden of Eden. And therefore, they don't believe that God loves them enough to bless them just because he loves them! What a quandary—what a pickle we're in!

God has shown us many times by giving us His blessings when we don't deserve them, but each time we think, *maybe this time He won't love me enough.* Not true! God's Word says nothing can separate you from the love of God. (See Romans 8:35–39.) Well then, if that's true—and it is—then nothing can separate you from God wanting to bless you either. So if you give to your children out of your love for them whether they deserve it or not, then understand how much more God will give to His children. He gives because He loves them, and not because they deserve it. And if nothing can take away God's love for them, then nothing can take away His desire to bless them. God is love. Those that believe that God is, receive what He has.

Sometimes in times of weakness, when we fear and worry, we feel as though we have little faith. Yet those times when we think we are the weakest, we are actually at our strongest! This is because we have to press in and fight harder to keep believing and standing on God's Word. Things of the Spirit are opposite things of the flesh. In the natural, we think that weakness will hold us back from growing, but in the spiritual, weakness can be used to move us forward. It is only when we are down that we get up and fight. There is no reason to fight if things are always going well! So what we consider weakness actually turns into strength as we fight and don't give up. This is especially true when we don't see the results right away, because it takes more faith to believe over a longer period of time. When we see the reward right away, it doesn't take much faith.

This is what Paul is talking about in Romans 5:3–5. Faith needs to grow and it can't if we get everything immediately. It doesn't take much faith to believe for one day. The bigger the faith, the bigger the mountain that can be moved. If we have little faith, we can believe for little things. We still limit God. But when we have great faith, we take the limits off God and believe Him for great things! The greater the faith, the move we can believe God for the impossible. An oak tree doesn't start out that way. It starts as a small acorn. It would be impossible to build something out of an acorn, but it's not impossible to build something out of an oak tree. With each victory, our faith grows, so that in time our faith is strong as an oak tree! As I was contemplating this, and I looked back over the years from when I was a baby Christian, I realized how much my faith has grown. I believe God for things now that would have seemed impossible to me back then.

As a child, we receive from our parents, but as we grow older, we like to be self-sufficient—to take care of ourselves. Sometimes we consider it a sign of weakness if we allow others to give to us and we therefore rob them of their joy in doing so. But in our desire to be "grown-up," we sometimes transfer that feeling to our Heavenly Father. In doing this we rob God of His joy in giving to us. We need to realize that as we grow up and become independent from our earthly parents, we need to do just the opposite with our Heavenly Father. As we grow in Him we need to become more and more dependent on our Heavenly Parent. The world considers dependence a fault or weakness, but God is pleased when we depend on Him.

I think that sometimes people wonder if it's all right to ask God for their needs. But if our children have holes in their shoes and asked for new ones, wouldn't we do our best to give new shoes to them? Then why would we think that we shouldn't ask God? In Isaiah 43:22, it says, "But thou hast not called upon me, O Jacob, but thou hast been weary of me O Israel." God wants us to ask Him for help. He wants to give us everything we need. We may also tend to go around the "back door" when we do ask God. Instead of asking Him for the thing we need, we ask Him to provide the *way* for us to get it. We also try to reason out what we can ask for. We need to stop thinking in human terms. And then we need to expect that He will do it. We also wonder if it's a need besides food or clothing, is it OK to ask?

Is God a partial God? He sees our hearts, and if our hearts are right in desiring God first, then he will give you your other heart's desires and needs. It's a lie of the enemy to put fear in your mind that you should not ask. If your heart is right, if you're abiding in Him, then your desires will be His desires for you. Do you like giving your children the desires of their hearts, beyond just food and clothing? So does God. In Jeremiah 32:41, it says that God rejoices over us to do us good.

During prayer one day, I felt that God was asking me what I wanted. I told Him of a need I had. All of a sudden I got a revelation that God would not have asked me what I wanted if He hadn't intended to give it to me, because He already knew what I was going to ask! Isaiah 45:19 states, "I have not spoken in secret, in a dark place of the earth: I said not unto the seed of Jacob, Seek Me in vain: I the Lord speak righteousness, I declare things that are right."

One day, God was teaching me about childlike faith and how He wants us to come to Him as a child with complete dependence, complete trust, not walking in our own wisdom, but complete surrender. A child is trusting, humble, and hungry to learn. A child can't wait until Daddy comes home so that he can be with his father. God wants us to not be able to wait until we can be in our secret place of prayer and fellowship with Him. A child accepts his father's words as absolute truth, never doubting, never questioning. God's Word is absolute truth. A child knows his daddy will take care of him. A child does not fear when his daddy is with him because he knows he is there for him. A child knows that his daddy will give him every good and perfect gift. A child knows his daddy loves him—no matter what. A father will leave to his child everything he owns, everything is willed to the child. God has also willed everything to us. He has already willed it to us on the cross. Many people don't understand this. They walk in poverty, sickness and fear. They know what God has for them in their minds, but they don't receive it in their hearts. Once they understand this, the enemy is defeated. God wants His children to know and receive all that He has for them. Don't we want that for our children? God's heart aches when He sees His children suffer needlessly. God asked me one day if I had ever seen a mother sparrow with her babies. She gives them their food, and they depend on her, knowing instinctively that she will provide for their needs. It's simple faith. Now if a sparrow takes care of her children like that, how much more does our heavenly Father take care of us. When people don't realize this, they live in fear. God's Word says in Psalm 37:25, "I have been young, and now am old; yet have I not seen the righteous forsaken, nor his seed begging bread."

People do not understand the capacity of His love. They are thinking in terms of human love and behavior. They believe that God will save them, but they question whether He'll bless them. It's for the same reason—love. They believe that God loves them enough to save them, but that they're not "good" enough to be blessed. No one deserves either, but God did it anyway.

Why do people accept the one and not the other? Why won't they walk in the fullness of what God has for them? They accept the one gift and not the other. This thinking is polluted and causes them to remain stagnant in their faith. Yet if their thinking will change, then they will allow God to work in their lives to increase and bless them. They will not be afraid of change. They will believe that God will take care of them from glory to glory. They will trust God to do them good. They will not limit Him. "O taste and see that the Lord is good: blessed is the man that trusteth in Him" (Ps. 34:8).

There is a fine distinction between faith and trust. The Bible says that faith is believing without *seeing*. Hebrews 11:1 says, "Now faith is the substance of things hoped for, the evidence of things not seen." I believe that trust is believing without *knowing* (what God will do). It is relying in His goodness to us.

If we just step out in faith, God will handle the rest so that His plans will be worked out. God just needs us to take the first step, then He will do the rest. It's when we believe it's our own power that does it, that's when we think it can't work. Once we realize it's not us, but God, we will no longer make excuses or say it's not possible. Things that are impossible with men are possible with God.

There is one important issue that needs to be addressed. Sometimes people only see God as Santa Claus. It is when we see Him only in terms of Santa, only talking to Him like a child on Santa's knee with a wish list, that we get in trouble. For then, the things we want are more important to us than Him! People with "gimme lists" only come to God when they want something. They "forget" about Him at other times. They do not obey. They lead "double" lives.

When God's children come to Him, He wants to help them and bless them. His children seek to know Him more, they obey Him, and they want to be pleasing to God in all that they do. Then when they come to Him and ask Him for their needs, He will give them every good and perfect gift, even more than they ask. You see, the difference is, people with "gimme lists" do not have a relationship with God. They don't really know Him. But those that walk with Him and talk with Him know Him. They don't think of Him as just a Santa. They love Him and want to know Him, and want to be with Him at all times. They depend on Him, and trust Him to do what's best for them. These are His children whom He adores. These are His children for whom there is nothing He wouldn't do for them. He is all, everything we need. When we love Him for who He is and all that He's done, when we put Him first, then we know that we can ask Him for anything and He will give it to us as long as it's what's best for us. We look to Him and love Him for what He's *already done*, not just for what He *can give* us. God's Word says, "But seek ye first the kingdom of God, and his righteousness; and all these things shall be added unto you" (Matt. 6:33).

Spend time with Him, and obey Him. Yield to His will,

appreciate Him and be thankful to Him. When you do this, when you make Him most important, then He will bless you with every good and perfect gift.

To summarize, in order to receive all that God has for us, we need to first believe that He is I AM. Nothing is impossible with God! Then we need to believe that He wants to bless us. We also need to know in our hearts that when we confess our sins, He is faithful and just to forgive us our sins and to cleanse us from all unrighteousness. (See 1 John 1.) We should not let the enemy put us under guilt and condemnation. We are all unworthy to receive yet we are worthy in His sight. We need to allow ourselves to receive. Then we need to read and declare God's Word, for faith comes by hearing, and hearing by the Word of God. We need to remember that faith moves mountains. Faith is the fuel. It doesn't take great faith. It can be small as a mustard seed, but it takes faith. Faith starts out small but is increased more and more as we see the fruit of it. Then our faith will become stronger and stronger each time so that the enemy's lies will not be allowed to enter into our minds. Then victory comes! We need to always remember that if God is the giver of every good and perfect gift—and He is—who are we to question why He would bless us?

Chapter 6

Anger: The Devil's Playground

*I*f you have ever been on the receiving end of angry, harsh words, you know what the Bible says is true—the tongue is a weapon. It can destroy a person and leave permanent scars, more than even a serious flesh wound. Words hurt our very being, our souls. From the time we are children, we've seen the damage words can do. These words will even form what our opinion is of ourselves. Words can be curses or blessings. The child's saying, "sticks and stones will break my bones, but words can never harm me" is a lie straight from hell.

Everyone gets angry. Psychologists will tell us to vent our anger and not suppress it. However we need to know *how* to express it and *how* to control it without hurting others. Anger, like love, is a choice. Anger, when out of control is like a steam engine. Once it is allowed to get going, it builds up steam and goes faster and faster and stronger and stronger. When that happens there is no room to consider the other person's side. It is out of control. It feeds on itself and destroys everyone in its path. It is the devil's playground.

Anger is self-serving. It is a controlling emotion. The devil controls you at that moment so you can control and destroy others. It controls by fear. It is used to get it's own way by putting fear in the other person. It is not fighting fair because it does not allow for the other person to state their case. Many times it will cause so much fear that the person toward whom the anger is directed cannot think clearly enough, due to fear, to even respond. When anger is used to control, it is an adult form of bullying someone so that the person doing the bullying will get his or her own way. Fear destroys love. The Bible says that perfect love casts out all fear. Since Satan is the opposite, it is also true that fear casts out love.

When anger is used to control, the other side feels helpless and hurt. Emotional scars and fears form that only God can heal. When anger is bullying, it lowers the other person's self-esteem to the point of where they could possibly have a victim mentality result from it. The person may become withdrawn for fear of saying or doing something wrong to set off the anger again. They live with anxiety, feeling like they're walking on eggs at all times. The person then will worry about what they say to anyone thinking they will say the wrong thing. They may think that they just can't speak intelligently to anyone. Their self-esteem is also lowered to the point of not having enough confidence to make decisions for fear of making a mistake. This will destroy intimacy if it continues over a long period of time. Then both parties need God to make them whole again. We need to be transparent before God so that He can remove the roots and heal us. If we would also ask God to help us to look at the situation from the other's viewpoint, it could be enlightening.

The only help for anger is to take it to God. He is the only one who can deliver. But you have to want deliverance, as well as be able to admit you have the problem. Just as an alcoholic needs to admit he's an alcoholic before he can be healed and delivered, so does a person who struggles with anger. You cannot blame others for your anger. Anger is your choice. Do not give the devil legal ground.

The fruits of the Holy Spirit are love, joy, peace, patience, kindness, goodness, faithfulness, gentleness and self-control. The fruits of the flesh are the opposite: adultery, fornication, uncleanness, licentiousness, idolatry, witchcraft, hatred, emulations, wrath, strife, seditious, heresies, envying, murders, drunkenness, and reviling. (See Galatians 5:19.) When Jesus comes into our lives, He changes us. But sometimes a root is deep inside and the devil can bring it to the surface if we don't get to that root cause and deal with it. Sometimes we don't want to give it up. Is it being afraid of loss of control? Power? Is it the past that hasn't been completely dealt with?

Anger out of control is abuse. It doesn't have to be physical to be abuse. Satan must really enjoy seeing us wound and hurt one another, and leave lasting scars that only God can heal. It's often very hard for a person who has fear, because of having to deal with an angry person in their lives, to see God as a loving, forgiving Father. This is especially true if the person with the anger problem was their father or an authority figure to them. It is easy then for the enemy to put guilt and condemnation in them when they fail because they see God as harsh and unforgiving. If their natural father was unforgiving and harsh, they think so must their heavenly Father be the same.

When a person of authority has an anger problem, it can

be especially harmful. Parents, be careful of what you speak over your children. Jewish fathers spoke blessings over their children and I believe even to this day, many Jewish children grow up to be successful as a result. A child who is constantly called stupid will live up to that name. It is a curse over that child.

Husbands, you are the spiritual authority over your wives. Be careful not to speak curses over them. First Peter 3:7 tells husbands to be careful of their wives, being thoughtful of their needs and honoring them as the weaker sex, because they are partners with each other so that their prayers will not be hindered. Speak blessings over her and you will see her move into all God has for her. It will be a blessing to you also.

When you start to get angry, tell the devil to get lost and ask God for the fruits of the Holy Spirit. Ask God to give you wisdom and revelation concerning the situation. It may be a communication problem. Men and women are different in many ways, especially in the way we communicate! Sometimes it's as if we speak a different language. Men think quickly, say what they're going to say quickly, and that's that. Women need to express their feeling and thoughts, and yes, even questions, while you listen until they work it out for themselves. That's the way they process things. Men tend to think that just because women are telling them something that they want them to come up with solutions. Women sometimes just need a sounding board while they reason things out in their own mind. This seems ridiculous to men. But remember when you were dating, how you would talk for hours? Remember letting her just express herself and just listening? Did you think she was asking you to solve everything then? Why then do you expect her to think like a man after the ceremony? Didn't you love her for who she was when you married her?

God is the one who can give us the wisdom to communicate well, and help us to be patient and kind with each other in spite of our differences in expressing ourselves. Wives who have an anger problem do just as much harm. For God sees the two as one. A husband whose wife uses anger to control has an especially difficult position, for he knows she is the weaker sex and naturally wants to honor and respect her.

The good news is that if we bring this anger to God, He can help. The Bible says in Romans 8:28, "And we know that all things work together for good to them that love God, to them who are the called according to His purpose." Therefore as God teaches us, changes us and delivers us, we are brought to a new understanding and a closer walk with God. God will use what we struggled with to help others in dealing with these same problems. We can now be a hope to others as we bring glory to God for what He has done in and for us.

Chapter 7

The 3 D's: Deception
and Dealing With the Devil

One morning, God was giving wisdom about fighting the enemy, and showing me how much I've grown in this area. It has taken me a long time to learn, and I still have a long way to go, but I am learning by talking to God in prayer. When it comes to dealing with the devil, Christians either don't believe he is a threat to them at all, like he's somewhere out in space just hanging out, or they are paralyzed with fear of him.

Before I became born again, I went to a church that never spoke about the enemy, so I was in the first category. When I started going to a Holy Spirit-filled church, I was at the other extreme: very fearful. Christians need to be aware that they are in God's army, and the reason it's called an army is because there's an enemy and we need to fight. But most of us do not know how. We are "easy pickins." I was too afraid of him to fight. I thought that if I just hid and did not rock the boat, he'd leave me alone. Maybe so, but then I am neither hot nor cold, and God's Word says that then you are lukewarm and not pleasing to Him. (See Revelation 3:16.) What good is salt without its flavor? (See Matthew 5:13.) So to be used and useful to God, we need to be bold. Satan is able to put fear in us due to lack of knowledge on our part. God's Word says, "My people are destroyed for lack of knowledge" (Hosea 4:6). God also tells us that He has not given us a spirit of fear, but of power, of love and of a sound mind. (See 2 Timothy 1:7.) So how do we fight the enemy? We fight with three weapons—praising God, praying God's Word, which is our two-edged sword, and by pleading the blood of Jesus over us. Some know this but they do not *know* it. In the movie, *The Wizard of Oz*, everyone feared the evil Wicked Witch of the West. But when Dorothy threw water on her, she melted.

God has given us weapons to use, and therefore we should not be afraid. When we use these weapons, the enemy runs. He cannot stand them. Why do you think he wants to steal your joy and your praise? Now, when we're under attack it's pretty hard to praise and if he can take your praise by putting depression and discouragement in you, he's taken your weapon. The times when I've noticed quick victories are when I praise God, especially when I did not feel like it. Discouragement broke quickly and the answer came.

The Bible says to bless the Lord at all times. (See Psalm 34:1.) There is a reason for this. It's not just because God wants praise for Himself—it's because when we praise the enemy flees. Things of the Spirit are opposite things of the flesh. Praise is for *our* good. If Satan can steal our praise, then he knows he has stolen our joy, and our strength. The joy of the Lord is our strength! When we give God the sacrifice of praise, we are giving an offering to Him. We are getting God's attention, and the enemy can't stand to be around us! Each time the enemy attacks, if we run to God and praise Him, the enemy gives up. When we use all three weapons, it's powerful.

Are you struggling with anger, sickness, fear, depression, and you don't know why? Have you been delivered from these things, but it seems that you are starting to fall back into them? Things in the natural are very often connected to the spiritual. Have words been spoken over you that were curses? Have you allowed the enemy ground in some way by your own actions? Because the enemy attacks with deception, he will attack in ways that make you think you are reverting back to your old ways. This is so that you concentrate on the natural, and not where it's coming from. For example, you and your spouse used to argue about finances, but have recently been able to discuss this issue, and then all of a sudden it seems like certain sentences trigger the same old issues from the past. It's as if even the words used are the same. Satan attacks in ways he knows brings up arguments from the past so that you focus on the past issues and never realize that's it's him doing it. If he can get you to believe it's your spouse's fault, you are blinded to the spiritual cause and blame each other. Then you won't even think to stop him. Pretty crafty!

God has shown me that we can't let our spiritual guard down. We need to be attuned to the Holy Spirit at all times. When bad things start happening, we need to ask the Holy Spirit right away to understand where they are coming from, and rebuke them! Then if we do this right away, it will be nipped in the bud. This is very hard to do. You have to learn to do it, for when anger or fear comes in, you want to go with the flesh. It has to be done immediately, before the enemy gets ground. Once you roll with it, it's too late. This means taking control of your emotions before they get out of hand and letting God take over. It takes discipline. We do this by recognizing the signs, giving control of your emotions to God, rebuking the enemy, and most important, giving God authority in the situation.

Here is exactly what we need to do:

1. As soon as you start to see anger, fear, health problems, confusion, depression, starting to come back, ask the Holy Spirit to show you and help you recognize where it all is coming from, and ask God to help you.

2. Stop and listen to the Holy Spirit before these things take hold.

3. Rebuke the enemy and give God control and authority in the situation.

4. Praise God that we are one in Him and that He gives us all wisdom and understanding.

5. Ask God to help us and give us the words we need.

6. Thank God that we are strong in Him.

7. Give credit where credit is due; don't blame anyone but the enemy.

8. If you can see these things and know what to do, it will stop the attack.

9. If you do the opposite of what the enemy wants, he'll stop for good in this area. This may take time and repetition to learn to recognize the signs and to be able to stop yourself from claiming the anger and fear.

So many people are walking around with such a feeling of heaviness upon them. They are weighed down with such oppressions. The enemy puts upon them a gloom, a spiritual darkness. I've seen many Christians walking in this darkness, not knowing how to get out of it. The answer is in God's word. It is a lamp unto their feet. But so many do not use God's Word. It has to be a part of them. It has to be with them, using it to cut through the darkness. It is their sword. It is like a laser light that shines hope. But they have to know how to use it. They may read it, but they don't *use* it. You can read instructions, but if you don't act upon them and use it, it does no good. The enemy is having a field day with Christians, sending depression, discouragement, oppression and despair. And Christians are receiving these things without a word and without a fight because they leave their swords and armor at church and go into the world defenseless. Jesus came to give people life and hope. Yet even Christians are living in despair. Jesus is the Light of the world. He is still the same. He still does miracles. He is the answer

As I was praying one day, God gave me the impression of a spider's cobweb. Spiders control the fly population. They trap them in their webs. They don't have to physically kill the flies; they let the web do the work for them. In this, God was showing me that flies represent the enemy. Our web is the Word of God. We don't need to fight a bloody battle to get rid of the enemy; all we have to do is use God's Word. It immobilizes him. We should not be arguing with the enemy—some of us do—that's hand-to-hand combat. Just immobilize him with God's word. Fight smart, like the spider.

When the enemy attacks and then we turn right to God and praise Him he is foiled. Remember, the deception lies in that when the enemy attacks, he attacks in areas that we have or have had problems in the past. This is so that we are deceived and focus on the problem and not the enemy who's doing it. It's deception so that we fight and blame each other and ourselves and not the devil who is causing it. It's all spiritual. Don't fall into the trap. It's so simple but very hard to recognize when it's happening. God has given us His words and His weapons. They are only effective if we use them! Satan is a copycat. Just as God caused the enemies of the Israelites to be confused and fight each other, the enemy causes us to be confused and fight each other.

We also need to be aware that anger is a choice. Fear is a choice. How do we choose not to be angry or fear? We do this by declaring God's Word in our situation, and by praising His name. When we praise God, Satan leaves because he can't stand by and listen when we worship God. We need to run to God with everything. We need to listen to Him. He will guide us and give us wisdom in all things.

Walls—Satan's Stumbling Blocks

Satan uses strategies to come against you. They are mind games. He tries to make you feel discouraged, guilty, fearful or condemned. He does this to try to separate you from God. But if you realize this, and run to God with it immediately, his plans are defeated. And just as God's Word says that all things work together for good to them that love the Lord and are called according to His purpose, God will turn this for good. What the enemy meant for harm to separate you from God will actually draw you closer to Him. So no matter what Satan does, he cannot win—unless you hide from God. Those people that never want to be separated from God cannot be. It is only those that hide that are separated.

But it is not God who separates Himself from people. It

is people separating themselves from God! They pull away from God. Those that love God and never want to be apart from Him can never be separate. For these people will run to God when fear, guilt, discouragement, or condemnation are put upon them. Then walls are broken down. Instead of the enemy separating them from God, what he does is draw them closer. He's not as smart as he thinks he is. God knows his strategies and God's people are learning them, too. He who is in you is greater than he who is in the world. Satan's walls are only as baby's blocks. Will you stand strong and kick them aside, or will they be stumbling blocks?

Satan knows these walls can also come between you and your blessings. For if he can make you feel unworthy of these blessings, then you will no longer expect them. As we learned in previous chapters, no one is worthy, yet we know that our Father wants to give us every good and perfect gift. (See James 1:17.) Miracles come with faith and expectancy. It is no coincidence that when we get a word from God, and our expectancy is high, the enemy will come and try to rob you of the blessing. He'll try to make you feel guilty or unworthy in some way to discourage you and put doubts in your mind. But even when we have fears and worries, doubts and discouragements, we can come to God with them. God is our friend (see John 15:15), and that is what friends are for! God sees our weaknesses, and He knows each one better than we do.

But He loves us anyway. He is our Father, Savior, and Creator. He knows us from before we were born. (See Psalm 139.) He is not a "fair-weather" friend. He knows that in this world there are trials. But He said we could cast our burdens upon Him. How can we do that if we only cast our material needs on Him and not our emotional burdens?

It's all right if our faith is weak, God can strengthen it. He knows there will be times when we are angry, frustrated, or disappointed. He wants us to give it all to Him. It pleases Him when we trust Him to love us enough to help us deal with these things. When we think we should handle them ourselves, it is pride and control. When we're afraid He'll be mad at us, we question His love. We need to take action. We need to stand strong, take authority in the name of Jesus, declare God's Word, tell the devil he's a liar, and move on to expectancy!

Trust God to do what He told you He would do, no matter what. He is God. He doesn't change. Don't let your miracle pass you by. If we submit ourselves to God and use His weapons (His word) to resist the devil, he will flee. (See James 4:7.) Each time Satan tries to play these mind games, to put up walls, remember they are walls of baby's blocks. They can be knocked down easily with God's word. Each time you do this, it will be easier and easier to get rid of them. You will learn not to be afraid of the enemy. Once you're not afraid of him, he loses control.

What you do when these spiritual attacks come in your mind will determine the outcome of the battle. So many do not understand this, that is why so many are wounded. For the mind, body and soul are all connected. We need to not only know how to fight, but we need to recognize when we're attacked and remember what to do when the time comes. So often we get so caught up in what's happening that we get "amnesia." As we learn, we will start to remember what to do quicker.

The way to fight is by praising God and declaring His Word. But it needs to be done immediately, before the enemy gets ground. The minute the enemy's biggest weapons—

discouragement, depression, fear, or worry—come in, rebuke them, and start declaring God's Word and praise Him for the victory! Don't let the negative feelings take hold. The longer you wait to do these things, the more ground the enemy will take until you're in the pit of depression and sinking deeper into it. We sometimes let the enemy poke and prod us and we just take it! God's army is full of crippled and wounded people. Satan uses fear to kill, steal, and destroy. If he can make us fear, then he can take what he wants and he knows we will not come after it.

David went into the enemy's camp and he recovered all. (See 1 Samuel 30.) If we fear, we make it easy for the enemy to keep our "stuff." It is like taking candy from a baby. We are afraid to go into the enemy's camp. Satan knows when you say give it back whether you speak with authority, whether you mean it or not, and whether you'll fight for it. Satan controls by fear. That's how bullies work. When a bully takes something from a child, the child can say "Give it back," but unless he goes after it and means business, the bully will just laugh at him. But if the child stands up to the bully, he usually finds out that the bully is a wimp. It's the same with dealing with the enemy. We cannot fear. We must go in with authority and get it back, whatever it is—health, joy, or finances! When we overcome the fear, we win the battle, and our "stuff" won't be stolen anymore. Take up your swords and fight!

God has already given us His weapons; we just need to use them. Many Christians do not understand. They go by their feelings, when things of the Spirit are opposite things of the flesh. When the flesh says to be discouraged, the Spirit says to praise. What glee the enemy has when he pricks us with a dart of discouragement and watches us self-destruct. Yet he is

81

but a roaring lion without teeth! Most people would laugh if a growling dog came up to them and when he bared his teeth, there were none. Use the swords God gave you. God's Word and praise will cause the enemy to flee.

The other thing that needs to be mentioned is that very often, after we get discouraged, guilt and condemnation come in. That's the enemy. However, it's what we do when it comes in that matters. When we are discouraged, talk to God. It's okay to let Him know how you feel. Encourage yourself with God's Word. It's when you wallow in discouragement that you risk harm.

The more we allow ourselves to go with the discouragement, the enemy will fill us more with doom and gloom as we go deeper into the pit of depression. Then it becomes harder and harder to get out of it. We feel darkness all around. God's Word is a lamp unto your feet. (See Psalm 119:105.) That means that when we stand on God's word, light will come in and it will shine on our path and direct us. It is the stepping-stone to take us out of the pit. Job kept his faith even though he was discouraged. We all get discouraged at times, and we all fall short. Psalm 130 is a good example of discouragement to the point of despair. And it also says that if God kept in mind our sins, then who could ever get an answer to his prayers? But God forgives. Don't allow the enemy to put guilt in because of discouragement.

When you declare God's written Word, the enemy cannot dispute it. He may be able to put doubts in your mind when it comes to a word you received prophetically, but not with the written Word of God. Declare prophecy to speak that which is not as though it were. But Scripture, the written Word, is declared to fight the enemy.

As we go through these battles, we may have felt weak or

discouraged. We should not be worried about how we felt. It's the action that we take that matters. As we stand strong and declare God's word, which is our sword, the enemy is defeated. We also should understand that when the enemy comes against us, he comes against God's child. Since we are abiding in God and He is in us, we know that we can speak God's Word with authority and that the battle will be won.

Chapter 8

Johnny Appleseed—
Don't Eat the Seeds

*W*hen I was a child and was eating fruit, my mother would always say to me, "Be careful you don't eat the seeds." In the Bible, Jesus taught a lot about sowing and reaping, planting and harvest. We need to plant, not eat our seeds. This is because the harvest is always greater than the seed. For example, if you plant one kernel of corn, a whole stalk will come from it, producing many cobs, each which in turn has many kernels. These days most of us do not plant our own vegetable gardens, so the concept is lost on us. We just don't think about it. People don't expect the harvest, they only hope for the harvest.

An apple tree produces many apples. One apple contains many seeds, yet it takes only one seed to produce a tree, which will produce many apples, year after year. Yet, the fruit is not for the tree itself, it is for others to enjoy, and the seeds to produce more trees. Producing fruit is for others. We produce fruit by giving to others. We give a kind word, money to the needy, food to the hungry. If we keep all that God gives us, we will not produce fruit.

A pomegranate is highly prized and is made up of all seeds. Yet in these days, many fruits have been bred to be seedless. They are made for convenience in eating. But how can we grow a grapevine when we have grapes with no seed? Some people are like this. They plant no seed and produce no fruit. It is easier and more convenient for them not to give. They are like the dead branches that produce nothing, like the fig tree without fruit. (See John 15:2; Luke 13:6–7.) They are useless.

There are those people who have learned the principles of sowing and reaping and are like the pomegranate, they have many seeds and they sow. The seeds they sow produce fruit in two ways. First, it produces fruit in the lives they help. This is in the natural. It also produces fruit in the supernatural, for God's Word says that whoever gives to the least of these is giving to Him. Then in turn God will give a harvest back to them, thirty, sixty and a hundredfold. This is so that they can give more, and so on and so on.

Most everyone has a special feeling for helping others at Christmastime. We know inside our innermost beings that God gave the greatest gift of all—Jesus—because He loved us. But our giving should not be seasonal. It should be at all times. When Jesus came, He came to us forever. What if everyone helped the poor at all times? There would be no needy.

We give because God gave to us first. We give so that people will know of His love. We give because we have God's heart of compassion for others in us. Everyone has the seed of love in them, but it needs to be watered to make it grow. It is watered by God's Word coming to them and by someone showing them the love of God for them. God blesses those that bless others. You cannot plant and sow and not reap a harvest. So often at Christmas, people give the gift without the love. It is rote, ritual, the thing that is done. But when we look to Jesus, the greatest gift, then we give out of love for Him!

When we give to our families, we give out of our love for *them*. When we give to the needy, we give out of our love for *Him*. The first is good, the second melts God's heart. It pleases Him. And when we please God, is there anything He won't do for us?

Very often, giving is a question of obedience. How many times does God tell us to do something for someone and we really don't want to do it? There is a war between the flesh and the spirit. In our flesh we really don't want to do it, but in our spirit, we know it's the right thing to do. If we die to flesh and do it anyway, and if we do it cheerfully, I believe the reward is greater. I have come to realize that sacrificial obedience reaps a greater reward.

During prayer one day, all of a sudden these words came to mind, "No greater love has man than he would lay down his life for his friends." I realized that the scripture in John 15:13 had to do with this. I asked God what He meant by this scripture. Is it just the literal meaning? God was telling me that it means we die to selfishness. It means that we pray for people even when we don't feel like it. It means that we give to them when they have a need. It means humility, to be humble and not put us first. God's Word says that those who desire to be first must be least. (See Mark 9:35.)

I was reminded of the story in Luke 14:7–11. Jesus was giving advice to the legal experts. He said that if you are invited to a wedding feast, don't always head for the best seat. For if someone more respected than you shows up, the host will bring him over to where you are sitting and ask you to let him sit there instead. And you will be embarrassed and will have to take whatever seat is left at the foot of the table. You should do this instead—start at the foot of the table and when the host sees you he will come and say, "Friend, we have a better place than this for you. For everyone who tries to honor himself shall be humbled, and he who humbles himself shall be honored."

Our emotions have nothing to do with giving. We could *feel* sorry for the hungry and not give them food. We could *feel* sad for the sick and not pray. We could *feel* like telling the truth and lie. It's not how you feel that is most important; rather, it's what you do that counts. It is also easier to be obedient and to help others when we're not busy or not wanting to do something for ourselves. When you sacrifice something you want to do for yourself in order to help someone else, you are offering it and doing it as unto the Lord. (See Isaiah 58.) It could be time, money, food, clothing, or even an encouraging word. What it is doesn't matter. Sometimes it is such a small thing that you don't even realize it, but God does. Sometimes the smallest thing melts God's heart the most, just like the widow who put pennies in the offering. Jesus said she did more because it was all she had, and it was a sacrifice. Nothing we give goes unnoticed by God. And in due season, we will see the fruit of it. For nothing is planted that doesn't grow, yet nothing can be harvested before its time. In due season, we will see the rewards of our labor.

When we give, it increases our faith. God doesn't need our money, but we need to give. Giving is more for us than for God. It is a step of faith. Giving releases our faith and it releases God to give back to us. It increases our faith to believe so that we can receive. We cannot receive what we cannot believe for.

I think it is important that I mention that sowing and reaping is not one-sided. We can't just sow and not reap. Many will not allow themselves to reap. They plant and plant, yet they think it is wrong to expect the harvest. God is a God of balance. Giving and not receiving is out of balance. You cannot give to God and then not give Him the pleasure of giving back. People sometimes have a misconceived notion about selfishness. They think that if they receive anything they are being selfish. God revealed to me the definition of selfishness. Selfishness is not sharing what we have with those in need. Selfishness has nothing to do with receiving what God wants to give to us.

Chapter 9

Wisdom: With It See Doors Open and Multiplication

*N*ot everyone has wisdom. Wisdom from God is a gift. However not everyone will ask or even want wisdom. They ask for things instead. If you ask for wisdom, then you will have the ability to get the things. But it also takes wisdom to know to ask for it in the first place. So all wisdom comes from God, even the wisdom to ask for wisdom!

When King Solomon prayed to God, God asked him what he wanted. Solomon's response was that he wanted wisdom to rule the people. That answer pleased God so much that he not only granted King Solomon's request, but God also gave him great wealth. That shows us the importance God places on wanting His people to have wisdom. God's Word tells us in Deuteronomy 8:18 that God gives us the power to create wealth. One of the ways He does this is by giving us wisdom.

He gives us wisdom in our finances so that we can have wealth to put back into His kingdom and so that we can be a blessing to others. Every decision that we make needs wisdom. Yet Godly wisdom seems foolish to the world. For example, the world says to keep (possessions). God's Word says, "Give, and it shall be given unto you; good measure, pressed down, and shaken together, and running over, shall men give into your bosom" (Luke 6:38). We don't think twice before asking a friend about a good stock tip, but we never think to ask God for His opinion. It seems too foolish to us. We tell ourselves that these things are things of the world. Why would God be interested? Yet He tells us that He cares about the very hairs on our heads. Many who have taken their friends' advice and not bothered to ask God for His have lost everything.

It's true that knowledge can be gained through books. However a book cannot give you answers for your particular situation. Books can help you to reach an intelligent conclusion. But even intelligent conclusions are not always the best way to handle things, for human reasoning can only take into account the natural and the things that are seen. Godly wisdom sees beyond human reasoning. Godly wisdom gives answers to questions not even thought of. So seek Godly wisdom. It is the unlimited revelation knowledge of God to His children—just for the asking!

The Answer Is Blowing With the Wind

No problem or decision is too big or too hard for God. God will always give us the answer and lead us in the right direction, even when we think there is no solution.

When winds blow, tall buildings move with it. They are yielding to it. When branches are flexible, they also move with the wind. When they are hard and dry, they break in the wind. If we are unyielding to the Holy Spirit, we break when the stresses and pressures come. If we yield to the Holy Spirit, we move in the direction He has for us. As we yield to the Holy Spirit, we move with the wind and see God's power in our lives. If we are stiff and unyielding, then when the storms of life come, we break. Tumbleweed blows with the wind. It goes where the wind takes it. It doesn't try to move against the wind, that would be futile. When people move with the Holy Spirit, they allow the Holy Spirit to lead them in the right direction. If they fight against the Holy Spirit's leading, they will get nowhere.

Things of the Spirit are opposite things of the flesh. What seems strong is weak. When we try to take control, we can actually delay what God has for us. His timing is perfect. God will always work things out in our lives better than we can. We don't always know the solution, but God does. God wants us to ask Him for wisdom in everything. He wants us to include Him in all our decisions. There is nothing too big or too small. He takes pleasure when we come to Him for His advice in handling our careers, our relationships, our dreams for tomorrow, our purchases, and financial decisions. When we allow God to guide us, we allow Him to do His very best for us. Godly wisdom is priceless. From His wisdom comes all things: safety, protection, health, and wealth. God tells us to "Lean not on our own understanding" (Prov. 3:5). Isaiah 55:8 states, "For My thoughts are not your thoughts, neither are your ways My ways." God will instruct us and guide us in every area of our lives. If we yield to the Holy Spirit, we will know God's desires for us, which are so much better than the desires of our flesh. When we do this we will be winners, for only God knows the beginning from the end. Then we will not have to say looking back, "If I only would have done it this way!"

I wanted to know the difference between wisdom and knowledge, so one day I asked God as I was in prayer to explain wisdom to me. Wisdom is more important than knowledge, for if you have wisdom, you will have everything you need. You need wisdom to know how to ask the right questions and how to know the truth and not be deceived. God is wisdom. He gives us the power to create wealth (Deut. 8:18), and then He gives us wisdom to know what to do with it. Wisdom is more important than riches. Without wisdom, riches can slip through your fingers. Wisdom is better than knowledge. For example, you can have knowledge to know how to *make* money, but you need wisdom to know how to *keep* it. God teaches us and gives us wisdom in how to handle our health, our finances, and our careers—everything that concerns us. When we give Him control over these areas in our hearts as well as our minds, then He knows we are willing to learn and be guided by Him. Sometimes it takes us longer than we would like to learn. But God is patient as He prepares us to receive all that he has for us.

The wise are teachable, the teachable become wise. That is when we ask God how to do things and then we are open-minded enough to receive His instruction. Are we there yet? Are we willing to let go and let God? God's wisdom makes rich. Acting on our own wisdom is pride and pride is foolishness. Pride thinks it knows it all. Humility is knowing you don't know. It is an openness and willingness to admit it and ask God if there is a better way. We need to come to the full understanding of who God is. His name is *Jehovah-Jireh*, our provider. He provides the way as well as our needs. He provides the way to meet our needs as we humble ourselves and admit we don't know it all. It's hard, yet so easy once we do it. So many of us depend on God to meet our needs, but do we really allow Him to instruct us as to what to do and how to do it? We all need to think about this. There is always a way to build a better mousetrap! "Ask, and it shall be given to you; seek, and ye shall find; knock, and it shall be opened unto you" (Matt. 7:7).

As we surrender and give God control of our lives, we become an empty vessel which He can fill. A vessel has to be empty before you can fill it. Then as He fills us to overflowing, we can be used as His vessel to pour out what He's given us to others. Then He will give us more. An empty vessel never runs out of oil.

Chapter 10

Healing

$\mathcal{I}$’ve often wondered why some people get healed right away, but for others it takes longer. We know from God’s Word that it is always His will to heal, for His Word declares, “Beloved, I wish above all things that thou may prosper and be in health, even as thy soul prospereth” (3 John 1:2). When he says He wishes this above *all* things, we can understand that he feels very strongly about it!

Most of the time, I believe it has to do with God’s perfect timing. There is a reason for the delay that only God knows. (It may be that down the road, we will be able to help someone else with the same problem.) Maybe we have to do our part to take care of our temple first. This is one of the mysteries we don’t get the answer to until we look back and see what God had planned for us. This was the case with my husband.

We knew God's will regarding healing, so we could declare His Word with confidence over sickness. Yet we still needed to ask God for His instructions for our particular situation. We needed His wisdom. "My people are destroyed for lack of knowledge" (Hosea 4:6). Bill was diagnosed with diabetes over sixteen years ago, and we had been praying and declaring and believing since that time. Although the diabetes was under control, and most diabetics would be thrilled with his readings, we still wanted him to be off the medications. For years he did not touch sweets. We had seen many healings that were instantaneous and wanted that too. He had gone to a nutritionist to help with his diet, but never had the results we hoped for.

One day as I was watching TBN, I saw someone that I knew had the answer. It was a lifestyle change of eating according to biblical principles. I wanted Bill to get this program, but he was not showing any interest because of all the other so-called "guaranteed" programs. I really grieved in my spirit because I just knew this one would work. But even though Bill was not interested it seeing it, God wanted him to. God did a miracle! One day, Bill came home early to pick me up to attend a banquet. He was the guest of honor, so he allowed a little extra time to get home in order that he would not be late. We had a few minutes before we were to leave.

Bill turned on TBN. Lo and behold, at that exact time, the program I saw at least a month ago was being repeated! But for this banquet, Bill would never been home at that time of day. Bill watched and liked what he heard. God prepared his heart, and he started the program. We started to see results immediately with the diabetes and high blood pressure! He lost weight and inches. His medication was reduced. It was definitely God's perfect timing. Sometimes we have to know what God wants us to do on our end. We have to know what decisions He wants us to make to bring about His will for us. If we are persistent in our prayers and don't give up, the answer will come. A few years before Bill started this program, God showed me a vision of him being stronger, and healthier than ever before. I just kept praying about the vision, claiming it, and declaring God's Word until the answer came.

Could God have healed Bill instantly? Of course He could. But He showed me that if He did, and Bill kept up his old eating habits, he would only get it again. Looking back, even though I wanted instant healing, I know God had a better, more lasting plan for his healing. He sees the big picture and we do not. We should never give up. We should continue to be consistent and persistent in our prayers. We should not think that God doesn't love us or has forgotten us if we don't get healed instantly. We need to keep confident in His promises and keep declaring His Word until the answer comes.

For others the parable of the soil might explain it. (See Matthew 13:3–23.) For some, when they get a word of healing, the word falls beside a path, so then the enemy comes and snatches it away. He does this by putting doubt in the heart. For others, the word falls on rocky ground. They hear the word and are happy, but when some old symptom comes up, they lose faith. The enemy wants to steal your healing, so he will put the same symptom upon you. If you look at the symptom and not the word, you will think that you were never healed in the first place. When the word falls on the soil with thorns, it is choked out. But when the word falls on good ground, when the people's faith is strong, and they don't give up, it produces fruit. Psalm 91:3 states, "Surely He shall deliver thee from the snare of the fowler, and from the noisome pestilence." We are protected at all times!

Many people, as they read this scripture, see it as just words in their heads. But when they *know* it in their hearts, they have the confidence and faith in God's Word that they are protected from disease. How do they get this confidence in their hearts? By reading the Word and then speaking it repeatedly. It has to be so ingrained in their very being that they know it as truth for them. That is when their belief is made strong. God's Word becomes as true to them as knowing the sun rises every day. God's Word becomes a shield. That's protection! That is when they won't believe the lies of the enemy. Then they know that nothing can harm them. That's strength. It reminds me of Mother Teresa, working with sickness all around, yet not becoming ill.

When Jesus went to the cross, He brought salvation and healing to us. In Isaiah 53:5, it says, "But He was wounded for our transgressions, He was bruised for our iniquities: the chastisement of our peace was upon Him; and by His stripes we are healed." We have faith to believe for salvation, and we accept the gift of salvation so easily, so then why don't we accept the healing part just as easily? Why should we believe for one thing and not the other? We believe that God loved us enough to send His son to die for our sins, but we wonder if He loves us enough to heal us! Yet He did both at the cross.

Sometimes it's easier for those who are new Christians to receive their healing, than those who are longtime Christians! The new Christians have a new, childlike faith. They keep this faith as long as they don't allow the enemy to come in with doubt. Many longtime believers find it harder to receive because they feel unworthy. They know they've failed many times since the first time they received Jesus. They know that He forgave them their sins at the very beginning of their Christian walk, but then the more they fail, the more unworthy they feel. Yet, it has nothing to do with their feelings. People know that they sin, and they know that when they ask forgiveness, God will forgive. But they sometimes think that even though God will forgive them, that He will still punish them. Therefore they think that their sickness is punishment. Then they can't believe for their healing. But in Psalm 103:10, it says that God does not punish us as we deserve. We tend to equate God's perfect love with our imperfect love. That's why we don't always understand how He can forgive and forget our sins. (See Hebrews 10:17.) It has to do with faith. Having faith in God. Faith in God to believe Him at His Word. God doesn't change, and His Word is eternal. Time cannot change it, nor death, not even if the world comes to an end. They need faith to believe that what Jesus did on the cross was done for *them.* They are not worthy, but God is. God wants us to accept all that He has for us: healing, forgiveness, love, peace. God has made a covenant with us. Our part is that we have to be in agreement with His Word and to believe that "with his stripes we are healed" (Isa. 53:5).

There is another thing that stands in the way of healing. It is unforgiveness. This leads to a root of bitterness. We discussed this in chapter 2. And this root is unruly. Just as the roots of some trees spread and destroy walkways, so it is with the root of bitterness. It spreads throughout the body, wrapping itself around each part. This root of bitterness is just as real as cancer, and it needs to be cut out. The mind, body, and soul are all connected. That is why God tells us to forgive. We should to do it quickly, for bitterness has a quick growing root.

When the body's immune system is strong, it can take care of the pollution and toxins that come into it. Since mind, body, and soul are all connected, when the body is busy fighting the root of bitterness, it cannot fight the toxins as well.

Its energy is spent on the spreading root, and all the stresses and tensions caused by it. The Bible says that a merry heart does much good, so it is safe to reason that a bitter one does much harm.

Love kills the root of bitterness. Sometimes people are hurt so badly that they can't love, no matter how hard they try. *They* cannot, but *God* can. When people are finding that this is the case, if they allow God's love to come in, they will see results. First the root goes, then the disease. So it's not *their* love, which they can't have by themselves, but *God's* love that does it. God's Word declares, "I can do all things through Christ which strengtheneth me" (Phil. 4:13). So many Christians are trying to heal bitterness themselves, under their own power. That's why they keep failing. They can't forgive or love even themselves, so how can they forgive or love others? As they look to God, then they will realize that although they are unworthy, God is worthy. It is Jesus who sets them free.

We should not accept illness. God does not put sickness on us; it is the enemy who does it. So many Christians just accept it, with out knowing that they can reject it. "My people are destroyed for lack of knowledge" (Hosea 4:6). Many Christians are fighting in God's army with blinders on and their hands tied behind their backs! Understand your adversary. First Peter 5:8 states, "Be sober, be vigilant; because your adversary the devil, as a roaring lion, walketh about, seeking whom he may devour." But our weapons are mighty. We need to realize this and use the name of Jesus to rebuke it. Everything has to bow to the name of Jesus. Keep declaring God's Word, pray and believe and never give up. Satan has been having too easy a time putting sickness on God's people without a fight. Do not accept the negative, doubtful, discouraging words or thoughts that the enemy, or even other people, will give you. Find people who have faith and don't doubt to stand and agree with you, and pray for you however long it takes, and declare God's Word over you. I personally saw this work when an eight-year-old girl went into the hospital to have a lump removed from her thyroid gland. The report came back as cancer, but we rebuked it and submitted it under the name of Jesus, declared God's Word, and also prayed that the doctors would realize that the report was wrong before they removed the thyroid. The very next day, the doctors said they looked at the cells again and they were not cancer! Praise the Lord. Nothing is impossible with God. He is the same, yesterday, today and forever. He still is on the throne and He still answers prayer!

One thing that I should mention is that we have to be careful not to believe the enemies lies with regard to our healing. Very often when people get healed, soon after the enemy will put the very same symptom or pain on them to cause them to lose faith and doubt their healing. Then they think that they were never healed in the first place. If the symptoms or pain return, rebuke them and declare God's Word. This is why it's so important for us to have knowledge of what God's Word says about healing. If you can't memorize some scriptures, write them down. I have included several at the end of this chapter.

In summary, we know that it is God's will to heal. Therefore we should not pray, *if* it be Your will. Would we pray for salvation by praying, *if* it be Your will? If we think that sickness is the will of God, we won't resist it. That's what the enemy would like us to think. We should also be speaking God's Word over us and not constantly speaking of our sickness. Words are powerful.

We have learned that there can be hindrances to healing, such as unforgiveness, unbelief, unconfessed sin and the feelings of unworthiness that stem from it, or not taking care of our body. We have also learned that we should never give up on believing for our healing. We can't expect God to heal on our terms and in our time frame, however while we wait, we should be consistent and persistent in our prayers. We should not think that God has forgotten us or that He doesn't love us if we don't get healed instantly. We need to keep confident in His promises and declaring His Word, especially when the enemy attacks.

Finally, when our healing comes, we need to remember to thank God and give Him the glory with our testimonies. God heals and our testimony seals. Revelation 12:11 states, "And they overcame him by the blood of the Lamb, and by the word of their testimony..." I think often of the story in Luke 17:12 about the ten lepers. They asked Jesus to heal them and He did, but only one returned to say thank you. Jesus asked where the other nine were. I wonder if they kept their healing. We should always thank God and give Him the glory for His goodness toward us.

Scriptures that tell us God's Word for healing:

> Beloved I wish above all things that thou mayest prosper and be in health, even as thy soul prospereth.
> —3 JOHN 1:2

> For I am the LORD that healeth thee.
> —EXODUS 15:26

> O LORD my God, I cried unto thee, and thou hast healed me.
> —PSALM 30:2

104

Who forgiveth all thine iniquities; who healeth all thy diseases.

—PSALM 103:3

But he was wounded for our transgressions, he was bruised for our iniquities: the chastisement of our peace was upon hem; and with his stripes we are healed.

—ISAIAH 53:5

Heal me, O LORD, and I shall be healed.

—JEREMIAH 17:14

For I will restore health unto thee, and I will heal thee of thy wounds, saith the LORD.

—JEREMIAH 30:17

But unto you that fear my name shall the Sun of righteousness arise with healing in his wings.

—MALACHI 4:2

And Jesus went about all Galilee, teaching in their synagogues, and preaching the gospel of the kingdom, and healing all manner of sickness and all manner of disease among the people.

—MATTHEW 4:23

Is there any sick among you? Let him call for the elders of the church; and let them pray over him, anointing him with oil in the name of the Lord; and the prayer of faith shall save the sick, and the Lord shall raise him up; and if he have committed sins, they shall be forgiven him.

—JAMES 5:14–15

105

Chapter 11

Hang On—Timing Is Everything

*T*he Bible says that before we were born, God scheduled each day of our lives. (See Psalm 139.) He knew our end from our beginning. He wants us to trust Him and believe that He has worked everything out for our good. (See Jeremiah 29:11.) Yet, we are an impatient people who want to walk in all that He's promised us—now!

God has scheduled a perfect time for everything. The sun rises every morning and the moon every night. The dew falls on the grass at just the right time to make it grow. Yet it's easy to believe these things happen because we see them. But faith is believing things that are yet unseen. God will tell us what He has planned for us in the future. (See Jeremiah 33:3.) We may believe that He's given us a word in prayer or through a word of prophecy spoken over us. We get confirmations on the word.

However as times goes on, we have to stand strong on that word and not give up. We have to realize that it is God's timing not ours, and His timing is perfect. His Word is true, it always produces. God has spoken everything into existence. Before time, He spoke us into being, but we were not born until the exact time we were supposed to be born. So it is with everything. Every one of His promises will come about when and in the time He has set. The words have already been spoken. The time is to come. It is like a time-release capsule. We should not be weary or faint, but we should wait on the Lord.

When we get a word from the Lord, we should know that it is coming and should not be concerned about when. God's Word is better than money in the bank. You know it's there and you can draw on it whenever you like. Nothing can destroy or devour it. It is your security.

God tells us the end from the beginning. He gives us these words to give us hope. As we put our hope in His hands, our hope is like a seed. When we plant it in God's hands, He makes it grow and gives us back more than we could imagine. God will tell us what He will do, but He usually does not tell us when or how. He tells us so that He can prepare us, so that we can take hold of it and declare it and stand on His promises. And then as we put our hope in God and we plant the seed of hope in His hands, He makes it grow so that when we see His promise come about, He gives us much more than we had originally hoped for. Ephesians 3:20 states, "Now unto him that is able to do exceeding abundantly above all that we ask or think, according to the power that worketh in us."

Promises, Patience, and Perfect Timing

So many times, God has given us a word and we wait and wait, and we don't see it happen. We wonder, did we hear right? Have I done something wrong? If it was someone else who gave us the word we question if he was really hearing from God. The enemy comes in to steal, kill, and destroy (see John 10:10), and if he can make you doubt, then he can go a step further and have you give up on the Word. Just as he told Eve in the garden, "Did God really say that?" He put question and doubt in her mind and then her reasoning took over. God will tell us what He's going to do, but He usually does not tell us when. He tells us these things are going to happen to give us hope, not to frustrate us. He tells us these things to prepare us for what He has for us. Timing is everything. But it is God's timing, not ours. It's not always immediately after He gives us a word, in fact it usually is not.

Very often, as we wait, we get impatient and try to help make it happen. God doesn't need our help, we cannot make it happen, and we cannot make it happen in our time. We must step back and wait—no matter how long it takes. If we try to make it happen, it will only frustrate us. Sometimes we're so focused on the promise that as we wait, it consumes us.

We need to focus on the Lord and not just His promises. When something is consumed by fire, it is burned up. When we are so consumed by the promise that we lose focus on God, we are *burned out*. We need to rest in God, knowing that He will take care of it. And He will do it better than we could ever imagine. (See Ephesians 3:20.) God will always do what He says He will do. He will work out His plans for you, but it will be in His time and in His way. If we try to take control over it we will think that it's our doing that made it happen. God does things in a way that we will know that it is He who has done it. So instead, we need to stand on God's Word, be happy and be thankful, being assured that it will happen according to God's plan and perfect timing. When God gives us a word, we should consider it done. He does not speak idly. When we pour hot water over a tea bag, we expect that it will be brewed. When God gives us a word we can expect that He will do it. We consider it as fact.

Anyone who puts his or her hope in God will never be disappointed. The Word of God says in Jeremiah 17:7, "Blessed is the man that trusteth in the Lord, and whose hope the Lord is." God's Word spoke the heavens and earth into being. When His Word is spoken it takes form. We should never be concerned about His Word coming to pass. What He said will be, will be.

One day when I was thinking about God's promises, I was getting a comparison of being on a mountaintop and looking down at all the houses. But then clouds rolled in and I could not see the houses anymore. Even though I couldn't see the houses however, they were still there. When God first gives us a word, we see the promise clearly. Then as we wait, we sometimes allow doubts or trials to cloud our vision. But the fact is that although the clouds in our minds are giving us trouble seeing the reality of God's promise, just like the houses, the promise is still there. They cannot be removed. We just can't see them at the time. If we stand strong on God's Word and keep believing in His promises, our faith will be strong, the clouds will break, and we will see the reality of His promise.

When we go through trials as we wait for the promise, we need to remain strong in our faith, looking to the promise and not the problem or circumstance. It is important that we do not look with our own eyes, but to look with Jesus' eyes because He sees much farther down the road. We should not go by our own senses, what we see in the natural, or what the enemy puts in our minds to affect our emotions. We have to be careful that we are not controlled by our emotions. Emotions go up and down like a seesaw. Our emotions go by what is going on in the world around us; they go by our senses. Faith is not controlled by emotions. It does not go up and down like a seesaw. It is as steady as Mt. Zion. As we stand strong, then when we hear God's voice, we will know without a shadow of a doubt that what He says, He will do, He will do. Then when things in the natural are not pointing to what God said, we will not allow Satan to work on our minds with doubts and discouragements. Faith is standing strong on God's word, even when things are looking different. In Romans 5:3–5, it says, "And not only so, but we glory in tribulations also: knowing that tribulation worketh patience; and patience, experience; and experience, hope: And hope maketh not ashamed..." Then we will have faith enough to trust God that what He says He will do, He will do. Worrying about it is so futile. God's plans do not change and worrying about it will not bring it about any sooner. So just trust Him and He will bring it about.

We also need to remind ourselves that discouragement is not faithlessness. Even in discouragement, Job remained faithful to God, and God blessed him double because of it. God does not get mad at us when we're discouraged. Satan just uses that tool to torment us. The enemy will make us think that if we have faith, we cannot be discouraged. However, as stated in the chapter on faith, if we are discouraged, yet still hope in God, then our faith is actually stronger at those times. It takes more faith to keep trusting God and to believing God when times are hard. Great faith is saying, "Lord, even when I'm in the pit, I look to You for the answers." David did exactly that. He was a man of great faith, but in the Book of Psalm, it also shows us how he was discouraged at times. The enemy will come to you with guilt because of being discouraged. Don't take the bait, for once you do the hook is in! Just come to God and take your discouragement to Him. He can handle it. You can trust Him with how you feel. His understanding is unlimited. He knows what you are going through. Then, after giving it to Him, let Him know your hope is in Him.

Don't give up! That is the key. If we have faith and we keep right on believing and don't give up, we will see God work out His plans for us. You see the promise is like a flower. First it buds, then it flowers, then a small fruit develops, and then it grows and has to ripen before it's ready to eat. So it is with God's promises. They will develop into mature fruit. The problem is that some are not willing to wait. Fruit is not edible if it is picked before its time. It is small and unripe. It has to be in season. It has to be the proper time. God's timing is perfect. For every time there is a season. (See Ecclesiastes 3:1.)

Many of us have waited for a very long time for our promises to be fulfilled. The longer the wait, the harder it is to realize that it will all come about. But there are several reasons why we need to wait. First, God needs to prepare the circumstances that will bring it about. He needs to put people and positions in place and whatever else it will take. Then He needs to prepare our hearts for the way it will happen. I can remember a friend telling me that he never wanted to invest in real estate. Too risky, too many problems, he was so against it! But God wanted to bless this man financially in this way. God needed to prepare his heart first and give him the desire to do it. Sure enough, the man is now investing this way—a miracle to those that know him. Looking back, this man saw how God, over the years, gave him the knowledge he needed to have before he could do it and then put people in his life to show him how they had succeeded at it. The third thing is that God needs to show us what to do with the promise. When God gives us a word, it is to work out His plans for us and we need to know what His purpose is for the promise.

Think of it this way. When a car is being made, no step can be left out otherwise it will not come together properly, nor will it work. Each one of God's steps has to be put in place before the promise comes about. As we are patient and wait for God to work everything out, we will see all the good that he has for us. And as we look back over the wait, we will understand what needed to be done before it could happen.

The important thing is to never give up. However, even if you have gotten a word and it's been such a long time that you've "put it on the shelf" or have even given up on it, it's not too late. Dig it up, dust it off, start believing, and declaring God's Word.

Chapter 12

Trials—Passing the Test, Or Retesting, Retesting— When Will I Get It Right?

*T*rials seem to be a part of every Christian's life. We don't look forward to them or even want them, but they seem to be necessary to our growth. When we go through these trials, the one thing God has impressed upon me is to keep my eyes on Him and not the circumstances!

It is when we look at the circumstances that fear comes in. God brought my mind to the passage of Scripture where Peter saw Jesus walking on the water, and he got out of the boat and started walking on the water, too. He was fine as long as he kept his eyes on Jesus, but once he looked down at the water, he became frightened and started to sink. Isn't that exactly what happens to us? How many times do we look at the problem and then we handle it wrong? We goof. I was talking to God one day about my doing just that. He asked me what goof is spelled backwards (without the double o). I realized it was fog. This is what happens to us when we concentrate on the problem. Fear comes in, and the fear creates a fog in our minds so that we cannot think clearly, or see God clearly, or hear Him clearly. We usually have trouble praying also. It is at those times that we may pray *to* God, but can't think clearly enough *to ask* Him what to do. After going through this, I had asked God, "How do I handle it better next time?" He told me not to panic, to stop right away, and talk *with* Him—not just *at* Him—and that I should tell Him what the problem is (which He already knows) and to ask Him about it. He already has the answer. But I also needed to talk to Him first, before trying to solve the problem and to give Him control of it right away. We should not look at the problem or try to control it (even by prayer) because then confusion comes in, and we run around like a chicken with its head cut off. Trying to control by prayer is by praying our own will instead of God's. Coming to God *in* prayer is giving Him the situation, telling Him we don't know what to do, asking Him to help us and handle it. Then God will let us know His will, or give us instructions and His peace will come. Then we will see clearly, no fog! Goof-proof!

We need to understand that there is a difference between controlling prayer and declaring God's Word. Controlling prayer is when we pray for the situation to be done in our own way, in our own time and without knowing God's will or considering His way of handling it. When we declare God's Word, we already know God's will and we are standing on that word and what God has told us. Controlling prayer doesn't ask God what His will is first, or doesn't care. When we lay out our needs before God, and we should, lay them down at His feet, ask Him to handle them, ask Him for any

instruction, ask Him what he wants to do in the situation, but
don't tell Him to do it in this way or that way. Trust Him to
handle it in His way—the best way. For God's Word says that
His ways are not our ways, His thoughts are not our thoughts.
(See Isaiah 55:8.) Then, as He speaks to you, declare it is so.
Ask, listen, then believe and stand on what He's told you. I
thought of how we teach our children to stop, look, and listen
when they cross the street. We need to learn to ask, listen, and
then stand on God's Word!

I happen to be nearsighted in the natural, but God showed
me as I was going through a trial, that I was myopic (He certainly got my attention with that word!) in how I looked at
the problem. He told me that I was being shortsighted and
could see only one way out, one answer. He told me that there
are answers that He sees that I have not even thought of. And
I should not lean on my own understanding because my sight
is limited. He told me that what seems so big to me, is tinier
than the head of a pin to Him. He just wants me to trust
Him for the answer, because He already has it all worked out!
He said that I needed to set my vision higher, which I under-
stood meant to keep my eyes on Him, from where my help
comes. Psalm 121:1–2 immediately came to mind, which says
"I will lift up mine eyes unto the hills, from whence cometh
my help. My help cometh from the Lord, which made heaven
and earth." He told me to remember that He loves me and
that when you love someone, you want to help them and give
them what they need.

Sometimes when we're in the midst of a trial, we wonder
if we'll ever get out of it. But we need to know that God
has everything under control. Even if the trial is an attack of
the enemy, God will work it out for our good. Romans 8:28
states, "And we know that all things work together for good to

them that love God, to them who are the called according to His purpose." God showed me that when He says "for good," it has two meanings. The first meaning is that when He works things out for us, He works them out in our best interest, with good things as the result. The second meaning is that He says it is done for good: finished, completed, and done. His plans do not change. He knows the beginning from the end, and we can be sure that He will work out His plans for us. Even when we step in and try to work things out ourselves, and we "mess things up," God turns it for good. And we know that in Jeremiah 29:11 it says, "For I know the thoughts I think toward you, saith the Lord, thoughts of peace, and not of evil, to give you an expected end."

At times we feel that we are alone and are left to handle the trouble all by ourselves. But God is with us even if we don't feel His presence. I thought of a seashell and how when it's out of the ocean, you can still hear the sound of the ocean in it. We don't see any ocean in it, but we can still hear it. Even though we may not feel God's presence in us at times, he is still in us and with us. There will be times when we are up and times when we are down, but there is never a time when God is not with us. We just need to close our eyes and listen for the sound of His voice. I remember one time in particular, I was grumbling to God about having to through a trial and I asked him why I was going through these things. His answer caught me by surprise as He responded with a question, "What's the name of the book?" I had to chuckle as I answered, *Lessons I Learned From the Lord!* God can make us laugh even when we don't feel like it. My mood changed immediately.

When I was praying one day about a particular burden, God was telling me how He feels our biggest burdens, our smallest cares. He weeps even when we cut our finger. He reminded me of how I felt if one of my children got hurt. He showed me that that is only a small part of what He feels for us. He sees our hurts, and He feels our pain. But with one touch He can make it better. He wants to just put His arms around us and comfort us. When we get in God's presence, when we allow Him to put His arms around us, that is when we will see victory so much quicker than if we just rattle off our needs to Him. When we make time to be with God, is there anything He won't do for us? That is when we break through the enemy's camp. Victory comes with God's presence. As we are in His arms, we see our need of Him. And as our hearts are next to His, He sees our need and takes care of it. In fact, it's those times when we are in His arms, that that is when He not only meets our needs, but also gives us the desire of our hearts.

We sometimes have trouble trying not to worry about and be consumed by our problems and needs. But God will always meet our needs. He will take care of them whether we worry or not. Psalm 37:1–9 says that we should trust the Lord, delight in the Lord, commit our way to the Lord, and He shall bring it to pass. It says that we should wait patiently for Him and not to fret or worry. When we focus on the problem, it becomes heavier and heavier. Then we become fearful, and it blocks us from hearing God. When we focus on God, we are brought up out of our cares. They become lighter as He removes them and we trust Him more. Then we can hear Him and listen to Him as He instructs us. God can handle even what seems impossible to us. He already has it all worked out.

When struggles come, that's the time when we need to stand strong on God's word. I think that sometimes the enemy will attack us especially hard when we're about to get a blessing.

He wants to delay or hinder it in some way. But if we stand strong and not give up, he'll eventually give up. We must continue to pray, praise God, and declare His Word out loud with our mouths and not to give up until the victory comes. When we feel overwhelmed, when things seem impossible, that's when God steps in. David felt this way in Psalm 61. He was overwhelmed, yet he declared that God is his shelter and a strong tower from the enemy.

The storms in our life aren't always bad, they can be good for us too—even though we don't see it as good at the time. When a storm ends, the sun always comes out again. Storms provide the rain that makes things grow. The storms in our life usually bring growth to us. It is not good to remain "status quo," to be complacent. But in order to grow, there needs to be a stretching—a change in us. Change is a good thing. Growth is a good thing. It changes our character to become more like Christ. When trials come, those not in Christ become bitter. Those in Christ become better. Life is a refining process, for to be with Christ, we must become like Him. We should not be dismayed then when the storms come, for we know that God will work all these things out for our good. (See Romans 8:28.)

As we are going through these struggles, and we do battle with the enemy, as well as with our own flesh, we sometimes don't realize that as we go through these things God is purifying and cleansing us so that He can use us. We don't realize that everything that is being taken out needs to be uprooted, so that we can be a clean vessel. We are growing and becoming all that God made us to be!

With each battle there is a victory, which brings us closer to God. After each battle there is a light that exposes any darkness and we become stronger, purer, and rid of another stronghold that would keep us bound. As we keep pressing forward and keep running the race, we get closer and closer to the prize. God showed me an example of this as I was praying about a particular battle one day. He showed me that salmon swim upstream to birth their young (their purpose). It is not easy for them. We must also run against the current (our struggles in the world), for the prize. Anything worthwhile is generally not come by easily. Perseverance is the key. As Christians, we need perseverance. When trials come, perseverance helps us keep our eyes on the goal. We hold onto God's Word no matter what, to get to the desired end. There may be times when we trip and times when we are wounded, but we get back up and keep running the race. It takes perseverance, and yes, even a certain stubbornness to not give up when these trials come. Stubbornness isn't always a bad thing. It is a good thing when we stick to the truth of God's Word and not allow deception to come in and lead us in the wrong direction. Stubbornness is a bad thing if we are so set in our thinking that we don't allow ourselves to learn and grow. I thought of when people run in a race. It takes perseverance. It is not easy to get to the finish line. Some quit along the way. It's like that in a spiritual race, too. We need to keep running even when the trials come. Sometimes it's so much easier to stop and be contented with what God has given us so far. But those that continue to run forward, even with the trials, get everything God has for them. God doesn't want us to settle for less. He has so much for us!

There are some in the body of Christ that are so weak and wounded that they cannot get up by themselves. That is why it is so important to pray for one another, to help one another in times of trouble; to lend a hand in times of need. One small hand to help them up can help them finish the race. A runner in a natural race will be offered a cup of water along the way to refresh him. We need to do that for others in their spiritual race. Those that are stronger can help those that are weak. In a natural race, it is every man for himself. In a spiritual race, stopping to help someone moves you along faster in your race. As I have said before, things of the Spirit are opposite things of the flesh.

Sometimes the trials that we go through are battles between our flesh and our spirit. As long as we realize that this is nothing new or unusual, we can have the victory! There will always be battles between the flesh and the spirit. We are told in Galatians 5:17, "For the flesh lusteth against the Spirit, and the Spirit against the flesh: and these are contrary the one to the other; so that ye cannot do the things that ye would." You see, we are in the world, yet we are not of the world. Paul tells us of this struggle in Romans 7:15–25. He also tells us the answer. In Christ we have the victory—our flesh has been crucified and now we are able to walk in the Spirit and not be controlled by the flesh. God loves us just the way we are. It is not a "license to sin', yet if we do fall short, we can confess our faults to Him and be free. He wants us to have peace. He knows our hearts and He knows that we *want* to be obedient because we love Him. That's different from *having* to do everything exactly right because of the law. We don't need to look to the law like the Israelites did; instead we can look to Jesus. We can look at His love.

Chapter 13

Faith, Hope, and Love, But the Greatest Is Love

*T*he one thing we need to understand is that we cannot understand everything! This is especially true concerning God's love for us. It is beyond our understanding—there is no way we can fathom His love for us. That is why it is also hard to imagine all that He has for us. God's heart is big. It encompasses everyone and everything. He loves the unlovable, the imperfect, and the flawed. Although it is hard for us to understand, He loves the sinner who has no idea of who He is, as well as those who are His children. But He is pleased with those who walk in His ways. His obedient children have His favor.

God was showing me that in the natural, the heart sustains our physical life in the body. It keeps the body alive. When two hearts come together in love, that love sustains the spiritual body. In the spirit, the heart is love. God is love, and when we are abiding in Him and He is abiding in us, we are one heart, one spirit, and one love. That is when we are complete. That is why people who don't know the Lord are never satisfied, always feeling empty, always trying to fill the "void" in them.

Even if we have everything, without love, we have nothing! Even if we had everything we wanted, but didn't have love, we would feel empty. Nothing can replace love. Everyone needs someone to love, and to know that they are loved. So, we could have everything and without love have nothing. Or, we could have nothing, but if we have love, have everything. Alone, our physical hearts can keep our bodies alive, but not our spiritual bodies. Only in connecting our hearts to God's heart, keeps our spirits alive and makes us complete. Love is one of the strongest forces there is. It is more powerful than many natural forces. Love can make the toughest person weep. It is what we crave most of all. God is love; therefore, we crave God even before we know it. I wondered why many people don't come to God even when they know somewhere deep inside that He is love. As I contemplated this, God gave me the revelation that it is for fear of rejection, being afraid of disappointment. There are those that have been rejected and disappointed by others so many times in their lives that they have lost hope. However God understands our frailties and faults, and He loves us anyway. God's love for us is unconditional. It doesn't have to do with our feelings, moods, or actions. His love for us is always there, no matter what. Jesus came so that no one would perish. He welcomes all who are lost, all who are beaten (remember He was beaten), all who were mocked (remember He was mocked), all who were rejected (remember He was rejected), all who have been wounded (remember He was wounded), and all who have been spat upon (remember He was spat upon). There is none that He would turn away. He knows what it is like to be an outcast. He knows what it is like to be treated as a criminal. He knows what it is like to feel unloved, even by His own people. So He cries out to the hurt, the broken, those who feel unloved or abused and says I love you. I welcome you with open arms. I will never forsake you. I will never leave you. In Psalm 69:5 it states that God is a Father of the fatherless. He also says that even if your mother should leave you, He will not. (See Isaiah 49:15.) There is nothing that can stop God from loving us. Romans 8:35, 38–39 states, "Who shall separate us from the love of Christ? Shall tribulation, or distress, or persecution, or famine, or nakedness, or peril, or sword? For I am persuaded, that neither death, nor life, nor angels, nor principalities, nor powers, nor things present, nor things to come, Nor height, nor depth, nor any other creature, shall be able to separate us from the love of God, which is in Christ Jesus our Lord."

Jesus is crying out to His people. He cries for us just as when He walked the earth, He wept for Jerusalem. (See Luke 13:34.) He wanted to gather Jerusalem's children together even as a hen protects her brood under her wings, but they would not let Him. He still weeps for His people today. If only they knew His heart for them. If only they knew His love for them. Who will tell them? His heart aches for them. His love abounds for them; there is no limit. There is no beginning, no end of His love for them. It is all encompassing, all-inclusive. He leaves no one out. The word *abound* means overflow, copiously supplied. His love overflows for us.

God's love is limitless. Just as we cannot see the end of the ocean, and it seems that it goes on forever to the naked eye, God's love for us has no end! One time as I was praying, the word *inconceivable* came to mind. It was then when I saw a large sphere shape. At that moment I got the impression God was asking me if I could tell where it starts and where it ends. He explained that that is what His love for us is like. His love for us always was and always will be. We do not ever have to fear losing His love. His love for us is inconceivable to us. His Word says that we don't know the breadth, and length, and depth, and height of His love. (See Ephesians 3:18.) No human can fathom it! No flesh could bear feeling it. It's inconceivable to us. People sometimes fear losing God's love because they have experienced losing a human being's love. But they should not equate God's love to any human love. They should never be afraid of losing God's love. It is as impossible as finding the end of a sphere. Being human, we will never know what it is to love someone as much as God loves us. If we could ever realize a fraction of how much He loves us, we would also never be concerned about Him wanting to bless us. We as humans, when we love someone, we want to give them everything. There is no end to what we wouldn't do for them. God's Word says if we want to give our children good gifts, how much more does God want to give to His children. (See Matthew 7:11.)

Many people are so afraid of God. Why? It is because they don't see Him as a loving Father. It could be because of hidden sin in their lives or possibly a cruel or harsh natural father. Sometimes people get frightened when they read certain parts of the Old Testament that show God's anger. The Old Testament shows what it is like with no Savior. But God loved His people so much that He gave His only Son for us. The New Testament shows God's love for us. I think it must hurt God when we see Him as harsh. When I was a little girl, my mother told me that if I disobeyed her, God would strike me with lightning. Up until that point, I felt Jesus' love for me in a great way. It was tangible to me. However after those words were spoken, I became fearful of God. After all, my mother was an authority figure, and all children think their parents know everything and can do no wrong. My mother had no idea of the impact this had on me until I told her years later. She felt very bad about it, but the damage had already been done.

We parents need to be so careful not to speak words lightly, and especially not to use God to control our children. It is like telling children that if they misbehave, Santa won't leave them any present, but in a much more dangerous way. I'm so glad God's love is stronger than words and that I found out the truth a few years later. The Bible says that perfect love casts out all fear. (See 1 John 4:18.) As I stated earlier in this book, the opposite is also true—fear casts out love.

God loves us, and He needs to know we love Him, too! He likes us to tell Him. Even though He knows us better than we know ourselves, He needs to hear us say it too. We like it when our spouses tell us of their love for us, even though we know that they do. So why should we believe that God doesn't need to hear that we love Him also? We usually don't even give it a thought. For love to be complete it has to be a two-way street. We sing a song in church and the words are that God is our heart's desire. He wants us to know that we are His heart's desire too!

People that love God want to please Him! They want to please him because they love Him, not because of legalistic rules. They want to be obedient. A little child so wants to please his parents. He wants their approval. He wants to do everything that's pleasing to them, yet he isn't always success-ful. But his parents see that he tries, they see his heart. God sees His children's hearts, too. The ones who try to please Him because they love Him, melt His heart.

But there are also those who try to please God out of fear of punishment. He loves them, too, but His heart aches for them. For it shows that they truly don't know His love for them. God wants His children to trust in His love for them. He wants them to obey Him just because they love Him, not because of fear of Him. He wants us to have joy in Him. Joy is knowing that our Heavenly Father loves us no matter what. Joy is not being fearful about not being perfect. Joy is confidence in God, His love, His protection, and His provision. Having Joy shows God that we trust in Him and His love for us. This is child-like faith. A small child, when he holds his father's hand, feels safe and secure. God is holding our hands and will keep us safe in His love. This is what makes God happy, when His children are secure in His love for them.

What gives God joy? I asked God this very question one day and this is how I felt He responded. Seeing His children happy. Blessing them. When His children seek Him and take time to be with Him. When they don't limit Him. When they sing to Him. When they appreciate Him. When they bless others because they love Him. When they realize He loves them for who they are. God loves all these things.

Hatred is the opposite of love. Hatred in a person spoils the love he *does* have for others. Just as one drop of poison will spoil the water in a glass so that it is not drinkable, so even one drop of hatred in a person spoils the love he has in him! That is why forgiveness is so important. Forgiveness is not being benevolent to someone, it is actually doing good for you!

The world has such a twisted view of forgiveness. Sometimes we get mixed up on what love is. There are times when God disciplines us because He loves us. He disciplines us because if we continue to do what we're doing, we'll get hurt. One day in prayer, God gave me an example of this as I was thinking about it. What if a child was on drugs? Would we continue to allow drugs in the child's room? Would we just sit by and watch? Would we say to the child, that's "OK, you can't help it?" Would we pray or would we also take some action to stop it before the child got deeper involved? If we truly loved the child we would confront it and take action to help him stop doing it. When God sees us doing something that would get us in trouble, He disciplines us too. He does it out of love. God will discipline us to bring us back to Him if we have strayed away or have backslid. He brings us back to Him through discipline because He does not want to lose us. God sometimes has to shake us to get our attention. When we step off the right path, He will get our attention to put us back on the right one.

God was also showing me another side of discipline. He was showing me that etiquette is very important—and that etiquette is being lost in the world today. Etiquette is caring about others enough to respect them. Etiquette is taught. A child isn't born with etiquette, in fact, just the opposite. To teach etiquette, is to teach discipline. Without discipline, a child will do whatever he wishes to get his own way, regardless of whom he hurts. Etiquette is genteel discipline. It is considering someone else's feelings and needs ahead of your own. People have gotten away from this. That is why there is confusion in this world. If it feels good, do it! If I want it, I take it! *Where is the discipline? Where is the respect? Where is the love for others?* Why is it that it is becoming "normal" to think what can others do for me, instead of how can I help you?

We as parents need to teach our children how to behave and get along with others. We need to teach them morals. It is so much easier not to teach them, but so much harder to deal with the results later on. Teach them love for people, teach them kindness to people, teach them respect for people, teach them giving—teach by example. Kindness is contagious. When we show kindness, they in turn will show kindness to another, and so on. But we also need to realize that meanness is contagious too. It is sowing and reaping all over again. The Bible says, "Train up a child in the way he should go: and when he is old, he will not depart from it" (Prov. 22:6). Isn't that what God does for His children? He does it because He loves them, and He doesn't want them going down the wrong path and getting hurt. He does it because He cares about us. He does it because He wants a good future for us. Isn't that what love is?

We very often only realize how much God loves us when we fail. It makes us stop and think how merciful and loving God is to us, even when we do things wrong. For everyone can love someone who is always good, yet God loves us even in our weakness.

As I was in prayer I felt God was asking me if I knew how much He loved me. With that, He stretched out His hands to show me the nail holes and said, "I love you this much". It was such feeling of love. I will not forget it. He loves us all that much.

Hope is the fuel, the gas that keeps people going. Without hope, there is despair. We give hope to people by an encouraging word, and by building their faith, for faith comes by hearing, and hearing by the Word of God. Faith leads to hope, but we need to have love to be able to share words of faith and hope to people. Faith, hope and love, but the greatest of these is love. (See 1 Corinthians 13:13.)

Chapter 14

Seven Words of Wisdom for Marriage: Exposing the 50–50 Fallacy

*B*efore our son got married, I woke up one night with these words of wisdom. I quickly wrote them down and presented them to him and his fiancée; however, I think they are good guidelines for however long you've been married.

1. Don't sweat the small stuff. Don't put importance on whether or not the toothpaste cap is left off. It's probably not about the toothpaste cap anyway.

2. If you get annoyed or angry (and who doesn't?), give it to God right away. Start thinking about all the good things about them and why you love them. Put yourself in their place, and try to see it from their side. You'll see your anger disappear.

3. Always show affection. This usually isn't a big problem in the beginning! Touch and say I love you often. Never take each other or their love for granted. Always let them know you love them and that they are most important to you in this world. Always let them know that they are your greatest gift.

4. Be a team. Have the same goals and be willing to work together toward them. Marriage is hardly ever 50–50. There are times when one has to give 90 percent and sometimes when that one has to receive 90 percent. Be flexible. There will be times when one's needs are greater than the other's. It is for a season and to accomplish a goal. It's a give and take!

5. You don't always have to be right, even when you are. Love is being able to say you're sorry when the other person feels wronged or hurt and you don't think you did anything wrong. It's their feelings that matter more than your being right. Love is most important. Love is a choice—anger is a choice. See the good qualities in each other.

6. Always make time for one another. Have a date night. Even if it's just taking a walk and talking. Send love notes.

7. Pray together. God sees you as one. When you pray together your prayers will be powerful.

Let Them Eat Cake

As I was talking to God about marriage and the chapter for this book, these words came into my mind. I asked the Lord what He was trying to tell me. He said that words are like food. If a spouse does not get fed at home, they'll go out for it. This is true for wives as well as husbands. We should speak words that strengthen and encourage. We should be each other's cheerleader. We should let them eat cake, which means to let them be nourished on loving, caring, sweet words. Don't feed them sour words that are hard to digest. Celebrate each other!

Chapter 15

You've Come a Long Way Baby,
But You're Not There Yet!

I have always tended to be an impatient person, always wanting things to happen yesterday. When I was a child, I wanted to grow big enough to ride a bicycle. Then when that happened, it seemed as if it was only short time later and I couldn't wait to get my driver's license. But growing in the Spirit is a gradual process, and learning isn't always easy. In fact if we don't learn the first time, God will give us another chance and another until at last we get it right. I've come to realize that I want to get it right the first time, because going around that same mountain is no fun!

I have also realized that the first step in growing and learning is recognizing the *need* to learn.

Sometimes we feel as if we're not growing at all. Sometimes the growth is so slow that we don't even realize we're changing.

In the beginning, when we first became born-again, the changes may have been very obvious. We may have no more desire to watch soap operas on TV. Or maybe we have no interest in going to certain clubs or to see certain movies that would have interested us before. But then as we grow, because the changes may not be as dramatic, we get discouraged and think that we are not moving forward. Yet as we take the time to look back at our lives to the place where we started our Christian walk, we see that we have been growing all along. For example, as parents, because we are with our children every day, we don't notice how much they are growing because it's so gradual. But if someone hasn't seen them in a long time, they are surprised at how big they are.

Children play and are not very concerned about whether they will be big enough to ride a bicycle some day, or drive a car, or do all the other things grown-ups do. They would like to be able to do everything older children do right away, and they accept that they will be able to do them some day. We also should accept the fact that we are growing in the Spirit and we will increase in maturity with time. We will learn more as we grow. Just as a child needs and learns maturity to be an adult, we need maturity to learn to hear God and how to handle what He tells us. A child doesn't learn everything he needs to know to be an adult overnight. It doesn't happen overnight in the Spirit either. God gave me an example of this by explaining to me about a forest. There were huge, mature trees, but they didn't get that way overnight. It took years. There were also tiny trees, which will someday be just as big, but that they need lots of rain and sun upon them to make them grow. We also need to be watered in the Word and for God's for light to shine upon us to make us grow. It takes time. We should not be discouraged. Patience and waiting can be a difficult but necessary virtue. It can be especially difficult because in the natural we are adults, but in the Spirit we are reborn as babies.

In the natural, we do not make the same mistakes as we did as babies. Yet in the Spirit, as new Christians, we will make mistakes. Just because we're mature in the flesh doesn't mean we are mature in the Spirit. It is a hard thing to swallow sometimes. It has to do with pride; it is humbling. There is always trial and error in learning and growth. God is gentle and loving as we learn. When a child learns to walk, he stumbles and falls many times. But the parent helps him up each time, cheering him on. God helps us up each time we slip or fall. He is holding our hand. We should be confident that He has begun a good work in us and will complete it. (See Philippians 1:6.) God will never give up on us—neither should we!

No matter how good our memory is we tend to forget how far we've come. A good way for us to track growth is with a journal. Then as we look back, we can easily say, "Look what the Lord has done." We see that we really have become a different person.

One way God changes us and helps us grow is by healing our "spiritual astigmatism." That is when we look at things in one way only—*our way.* I think we all have a little bit of the Archie Bunker type of thinking in us in some area or another. Archie Bunker is set in his ways and he sees his way as the only right way. Sometimes we don't even realize that we have this. It could be that we think that our denomination is the only true denomination and everyone else's is wrong. It could be that we think that our way of worship is the right way, or that our music is better therefore other music cannot praise God as good as ours. However as we grow and allow the Holy Spirit to fill us more and more, the old way of thinking goes.

We become new in our thinking as God reveals more of Himself to us. He expands our horizons and changes our perceptions as we see things through the eyes of His understanding and not our own human reasoning, which is limited. It is then that we walk in the Spirit and not in the flesh. When I was a child, I thought like a child. (See 1 Corinthians 13:11.) With our expanding technology and transportation, and as our world becomes smaller, our horizons are expanding as we learn about other cultures and how they live and worship God. We then have an appreciation for different cultures and the diversity of people of those cultures. I am reminded of a song I learned in Sunday school when I was very young—red and yellow, black and white, they are precious in His sight, Jesus loves the little children of the world. We are all His children—He loves us all.

It stands to reason that if we are willing to learn, that we will grow faster. We also need to learn to be willing to be corrected. That's a little harder. However no one who God uses comes to being His vessel by immediately walking in perfection.

There are many lessons to be learned! Are you willing? It is all a part of growing. Each lesson moves us into a new level of growth. God uses those who are willing to go through the process. It's not that they are perfect, but they have a pure heart and they try their best to do what is right, to please Him. They do this not because of the law, but because they love Him. God is drawn to them, and He picks them out one by one. They are His jewels, His treasures. Their hearts are like diamonds, transparent before Him. They are precious in His sight. A heart that is pure and clean has nothing to hide. It is crystal clear. Light shines through it. It is like a stream, when the water is pure, you can see the bottom. When the stream is polluted, it is muddy. You can't see the bottom, and you don't want to go in it. Rivers of living water come from a pure heart. The water brings and supports life. It all starts in the heart. God looks for those whose hearts are right with Him. It's not that the heart is never flawed, but any flaw that comes in is confessed right away so that the flaw disappears and the heart is clear again. As we grow we learn to keep short accounts so that we be able to be all that God wants us to be.

As we learn and grow, we are being perfected. We also know that perfection only comes when we're in heaven. I know that I still am learning, and I still have a long way to go. I'm "not there yet," but I'm getting better.

Chapter 16

Death—The Beginning, Not the End

$\mathcal{S}$ometimes when we pray for someone and they don't get healed, we wonder if we could have prayed harder, or better. We wonder if we could have done something else that perhaps we failed to do. As I wondered about this, God explained to me that sometimes when we pray for people to be healed, it is His will to take them home to be with Him. We must realize that it has nothing to do with whether we prayed in a good enough way, or said the right words, or had enough faith. He showed me that just because someone doesn't get healed in the natural, the way we want, we shouldn't feel as if we've done a bad job of praying. It has nothing to do with us; it is God who does it. He showed me that sometimes the best healing is to be in heaven—it's the *ultimate healing*. For when we go to be with Him, there is no sickness, sorrow, loneliness or pain. God wants us to realize this as we pray for the sick and sometimes we don't get the answer *we* want. We should not feel discouraged or carry a burden that we didn't pray "good enough."

God was teaching me about death, and He sometimes teaches me by giving me comparisons. He showed me that our life is our job on earth, and everyone has a specific job or calling. But just as we go to our earthly job every day, and we're happy to come home at the end of the day, after our life's job is done on earth, we're happy to go home to heaven. People need to know that it is the ultimate healing and that it's a time for rejoicing. We are sad and will miss them here on earth, but we also rejoice that they are with Jesus and we will see them again in heaven. The flesh mourns; the Spirit rejoices. Too many Christians take the worldly view of death, that death is the end. But death is not the end; it is just the beginning.

Then God gave me another comparison. This time I was being shown a beach by the ocean. A seashell was on the sand. He told me to listen to the seashell, and I heard the ocean in it. He explained that even though the seashell is out of the ocean, we are still able to hear the sound of the ocean in it. Just as we are now living in this world, we are not of this world. That He is in us, and if we listen, we can hear His voice. However someday, we will be "back in the ocean," home where we belong with Him. Death is the beginning, not the end.

People get angry with God sometimes when a loved one dies before what they consider is that person's "time." But God's timing is perfect; ours is not. And even the shortest life has had a purpose. We think in human terms of all the things they've missed. We need to understand that maybe God has prevented them from going through worldly sufferings. Only

God knows what that person would have had to endure. I believe that one reason God brings people home early is to save them from suffering. Our agony at losing them may have been far less than theirs would have been. This is confirmed in Isaiah 57:1 that says the godly perish, and no one seems to realize that God has taken them away from the evil that lies ahead "Come unto Me all ye who are heavy laden and I will give you rest."

God speaks life always; however, it may be life on earth or it may be life in heaven. Either way, it's life.

If you have never given you life to Jesus, pray this prayer:

> Lord Jesus, I believe that You are the Son of God, and that You died on the cross for my sins. I ask You to forgive me of all my sins. Come into my life, be my Lord and Savior, and I will follow You all the days of my life. Thank You for giving me eternal life, and thank You that now I am born again, amen.

Now if you have prayed this prayer in your heart, you have eternal life. It doesn't matter if you don't "feel" different right away; just receive the gift of salvation by faith! For it is by having faith and receiving God's grace that you are saved. Confess it with your mouth. Tell someone about the wonderful gift of eternal life that you have received and that you are "born again." Then get a Bible and read God's Word every day. Go to a Holy Spirit filled, Bible-believing church and get to know others in the family of Christ. This is the first day of your new life—a new beginning!

> May the Lord bless thee and keep thee. The Lord make his face shine upon thee, and be gracious unto thee. The Lord lift up his countenance upon thee, and give thee peace.
> —Numbers 6:24–26